THE INADVERTENT CAFÉ

Lessons in Life, Business, and the Limited Value of Being a Do-Gooder.

BY BRENT OLSON

Kirk House Publishers
Minneapolis, Minnesota

The Inadvertent Café:
Lessons in Life, Business,
and the Limited Value of Being a Do-Gooder
by Brent Olson

Edited and Designed by Cheryl Rainford, Four O'Clock Freelance, LLC
Cover photo hbpictures/Shutterstock
ISBN 978-1-933794-87-7

Kirk House Publishers, PO Box 390759, Minneapolis, Minnesota 55439
Manufactured in the United States of America

Lately I've been thinking about how much of the luck in my life has come at the hands of various women. From my mother, to my sisters, my wife, my daughters and my wonderful granddaughters, I owe so much to the women I love. Furthermore, there are the women I admire. So, to Lois Torgerson, the first person to publish my work, to Cheri Zagurski, the first person to pay me for my work, to Betsy Freese, the first person to depend on my work, and to Cheryl Rainford, the first person to advocate for my work AND make it better, my profound thanks.

— *Brent Olson*

Foreword

Brent Olson is a master storyteller—and a sneaky theologian. I've used his essays in my theology classes for years now; students think I'm giving them a break from "real theology," and are surprised to discover the theological punch Olson can deliver in what first appears to be a straightforward (and clever, and fun, and engaging) account of everyday events in rural Minnesota.

"The Inadvertent Café" takes both his storytelling and his theological insight to new heights.

I can't wait to share this book with my classes, and to use it as a springboard to discuss love, hope, mercy, courage—and most importantly, to explore the joys and sorrows, dreams and disappointments, daily chores and daily miracles that mark the work of building community and pursuing justice in our broken yet oh-so-beautiful world.

Colleen Carpenter
Associate Professor of Theology
St. Catherine University
Minneapolis-St Paul, Minnesota

Contents

Introduction

It's 8.7 miles from my house to where I work. It takes me between ten and eleven minutes, unless my playlist lands on "Pink Cadillac" or "Highway to Hell." That can knock about 30 seconds off the trip.

I try to leave the house by 5:35 a.m. That's pretty early. I get dressed in the dark, (socks in the top drawer, white on the left, black on the right, underwear in the second drawer, boxers on the left, t-shirts on the right), check the headlines and go out the door. There's a covered walkway from the house to the garage.

Usually, I get almost to my wife's car before the motion detector turns the garage lights on. Our giant Newfoundland sleeps on an old couch in the front of the garage, so I make a little race out of it to see if I can surprise her before she wakes up and comes to greet me.

I always lose.

I prefer to see it not as a loss, but as my contribution to the dog's self-esteem. She's a rescue dog—purchased originally to be a guard dog, until she never stopped growing, and wagged her tail at every intruder. I don't know if her pleasant demeanor or ginormous size were what led to her discharge from the guard dog business, but be that as it may, she was kicked to the curb. Due to her early trauma, my wife has diagnosed her with reactive attachment disorder. I see her as just a pain in the ass.

The commute is not always fun. In the winter, the heater doesn't start blowing warm air until about the time I pass the old Monnen place, two miles from my house. The family moved away thirty years ago. All the buildings have been gone for a decade or more, but that's still the easiest way to describe the intersection, at least to locals. Two miles isn't very far, but it can seem like a long way when you're trying to hold your breath to avoid frosting up the windshield.

During the spring and fall I sometimes have to factor in a little extra time in case of traffic jams. One morning I had to slow down for three raccoons, four deer, and a family of skunks waddling casually down the middle of the road. It's tough to drive around a skunk family in the middle of the road, and it's certainly nothing you want to do with your window down.

Summer is the easiest commute. It's usually light out and seeing the moonset or the sunrise over the vast expanse of prairie is a sight that I've never grown tired of.

Cal is often the first one through the door. Some days it's Randy, or a random truck driver, or a guy on the morning shift at the power plant. If it's Cal we usually talk sports, unless it's trapping season. If it's Randy we usually talk about our kids. If it's someone else we start the conversation with the weather, then daintily shift towards politics if it seems possible to find some common ground. For the past few months it's been Lester.

Lester is 88, and has a number of health issues, but he comes to town every morning around 5:30 a.m. to walk a half-mile on the treadmill at the exercise center. Then he comes next door to my place and has a cup of coffee while his pulse settles back to normal.

Not only is it almost always someone I know, but usually it's someone whose family has been friends with my family for three generations. There are exceptions—Phil, the new school superintendent, stops in early some mornings, but I don't know if he's in for the long haul or not— my hometown is a place where many people come just long enough to get the first lines on the resume and then move to a place where you can get a decent bagel.

I try to come through the door at 5:45 a.m. That gives enough time for the grill to warm up and a pot of coffee to brew. It's easy in June and July, when my eyes pop open with bird songs and sunlight. It feels foolish in January and February when the stars are still bright and cold, and a hard wind swirls down an empty Main Street. Still, I have an overdeveloped sense of responsibility, and the sign says, "Open at 6:00 a.m." so, well, there I am.

It's a strange place to find myself at the age of 60. My beard smells like bacon and my hands smell like soap. I fret about expiration dates on pancake batter and whether or not people are getting tired of ginger-molasses muffins with cream cheese frosting.

The place has been a café since 1926. The Masonic Lodge spent nearly $12,000 to build the building, then rented out half of the ground floor to a brother Mason who originally opened it as The Temple Café. The Masonic Temple took up the whole second floor. For most of my life, the other half was a drugstore. Now it's a fitness center, and the top floor is abandoned.

Before I got involved, the café had been closed for a couple of years. I only got involved because my father said, "You should do something to try and keep Bonnie's open." Bonnie's is the grocery store across the street.

At the time a group of do-gooders, (yeah, I know that sounds pejorative, but don't take it that way) were trying to get the building back into use. They'd cleaned and painted and then their efforts had ground to a halt. As my contribution to the project (being a bit of a do-gooder myself) I'd offered to put a new ceramic tile floor in the kitchen, with the hopes of bringing the facility within eyeshot of being up to code for the first time in fifty years or so.

As often happens in my life it had turned into a "thing." I had to tear a partition down and put in a new subfloor, and at this point in my life if I wish to walk the next day I can only spend about three hours at a time working on my knees. That meant I spent the better part of one winter alone in the building, puzzling over just what you could do to make this building a going concern, and fulfill my father's mandate.

Bonnie's has been a grocery store about as long as the café has been a café. I've lost track of the number of owners, but each one faced a larger struggle as the town's population shrank, and people grew used to driving long distances for food, and wanted more variety than a small town store can afford to stock.

That's the way the world works; businesses start, grow, flourish then die.

The two problems with that are: one, Bonnie is a nice lady who is nice to my parents and they hate to see her struggle; and two, the people who need the grocery store really need the grocery store. In a town of a little over four hundred people probably half of them are too elderly to drive very far or, for one reason or another, don't have a car or have lost their license to drive. Without Bonnie's their diet shrinks to what you can buy at a convenience store. It's a problem that's more common than you'd think, and what's interesting is that it's a problem that is most common in rural areas and the inner city.

Enter the Bush Foundation. In 1914 Archibald Bush was a bookkeeper working for Minnesota Mining and Manufacturing. In 1953 he used $200 million in 3M stocks to establish a foundation to "be a catalyst for the courageous leadership necessary to create sustainable solutions to tough public problems and ensure community vitality." One fine day I put on my blue blazer (so I would look professional), but no tie (so I wouldn't look like I was sucking up), and presented myself and my idea. In the end, I had to let business casual slide a little because the first thing I'd done in the morning was spill a latte over my clean blue shirt, so I had to keep the blazer buttoned.

What I told them was that as far as I was concerned there were four problems with food in a small town. First, it's hard for small grocery stores to stay open because of our mobile society and resulting competition from huge chains stores. Second, if you're old or not mobile, it can be very difficult to get decent food, simply because you can't travel to where the good, cheap stuff is. Third, there is a lack of interesting food in small towns. I'm not blaming anyone for that, but if you want Thai food for lunch, you better leave home around breakfast time. Fourth, if you want to produce food, real food not just commodities, there are tremendous barriers to getting into the business because of costs and regulations.

There may well be other problems, including the shortage of decent bagels, but those are the four that have bothered me the most in my six decades of small town living. I'm not much a fan of the "good old days," school of philosophy, because I like that there are titanium knees and girls' sports. Having said that, one of the pains of living in the same place for a very long time is being able to see the transition to something smaller, something not quite as nice. I imagine if I lived in San Francisco I'd be whining about the high cost of housing, and if I lived in Florida I'd remember the good old days before there were giant pythons hanging from the highway overpasses.

The solution I came up with was to open the café as a café for breakfast, from 6:00 to 10:00 a.m., and then have the licensed, up-to-code, fully equipped kitchen, available for people to use to make value-added products that could be sold at Bonnie's. Hopefully when people came in for the locally made cheese and organic salsa, they'd also buy some milk and eggs. Bonnie's would stay open, people would have better food, and a few jobs might be created in a place where the usual farm isn't considered full time work until it reaches a couple of thousand acres.

Evidently sloppiness was not a disqualifier, because the Bush folks said they'd let me spend $75,000 to see if I had a good idea or not. It wasn't until I started doing a final budget that I uncovered a significant stumbling block. The grant was a lot of money, but it was not that much money. It cost $12,000 to hook up the stove hood, I needed a dishwasher and some other equipment.

After adding things up I looked at my wife and said, "You know, if I want to do the things I want to do here I can't afford to hire someone to run this place."

My wife gave me a look of complete conviction and said, "Well then buddy, you better learn how to cook. Because I have a job."

This was an issue. I lead kind of a complicated life. First, I'm a writer. Many people don't really consider that a real job, but I do get paid for it so I need to take it seriously. My syndicated column, "Independently Speaking," is seen by about a million people a week and I really want to give them all something worth reading. That requires spending anywhere from one hour to two days a week staring at a mostly blank computer screen.

I'm also a county commissioner, which means I'm one of five elected officials responsible for the roads, and the Veteran's Service Officer, and the Sheriff's department budget, and Family Services, and the fairgrounds, and Toqua Park, and getting decent broadband in the county, and keeping the Treasurer's and Recorder's offices in today's technology, and some other stuff. It's also not a real job, and per hour it pays considerably less than writing. Along with my parents, my wife and I own about a thousand acres of farmland, which needs to be managed and improved. Last but not least I'm a father and grandfather with children who are always buying houses in need of remodeling, and their children are in school plays and taekwondo tournaments. My schedule is very full, but, here's the thing, it's pretty flexible.

So I learned how to cook.

I bought Mark Bittman's book "How to Cook Everything" and cooked all the meals at home for about six months. Then, even though I was still having a few omelet issues, on March 4, 2013 I opened The Inadvertent Café.

The name was easy. When I'd meet someone and they'd ask, "What are you doing these days?" I'd say, "Well, it appears that I'm inadvertently running a café."

Voila.

It wasn't as easy as it sounds. There was a group that had been interested in getting the café open. I'm not going

to mention the name, because they're good people doing
work they believe in, and the fact that they made my life a
living hell doesn't change that. I had worked with them on
several small projects, trying to smooth their way through
local politics. They're the ones who had started the reno-
vation project on the café, but their work had stalled after
they'd cleaned and painted. There had been a year or more
with no progress at all. The organizer called a meeting
for all people passionate about fixing up the café and two
people showed up, both of whom said, "Someone should
do something."

I ran my idea past them and no one had anything
better to offer. Their funding was running out and they'd
decided to let their lease expire.

After the Bush Foundation came through and made me
a Bush Fellow, word spread that I'd received a $75,000 grant
to renovate and reopen the café, which wasn't strictly true.
I had received a Bush Foundation Leadership Development Fellowship, which had $75,000 in funding attached to
it. I was expected to travel, study, do all sorts of stuff with
the money. The Bush Foundation saw the café basically as
a homework project for me, to teach me some of the finer
nuances of what works in local economic development. So,
the rumors were not really accurate.

The group called a meeting and this time instead of
two, about twenty-five people showed up, many of whom I
didn't even know. The vast majority of them were from out
of town. I gave my explanation, and then they split up into
groups to discuss how best to use the money. Two days later I received an email saying they'd conducted a telephone
poll and selected a governing board to help determine how
the money should be spent.

I sighed deeply, because there is nothing I hate more,
or am worse at, than dealing with conflict. I even con-

tacted the Bush people and asked them what they thought of the idea and they said, "Absolutely not." Since it was their money that seemed to be the end of it, as far as I was concerned. The group was pretty angry. In fact, as I write this, almost three years after I first opened the doors, none of the people who were at that meeting have purchased so much as a cup of coffee at the café.

It didn't help that at about this same time, in my role as a county commissioner, I had entered into conflict with many of the same people over a zoning issue. A guy who owned some land with granite on it wanted to open a quarry. There's a reason this is called Big Stone County, and quarrying is an old established business here. I didn't think this particular plan was a good idea, but it was a *legal* idea, a nuance that I had trouble conveying. At a Planning and Zoning meeting, a Native American college professor from Vancouver called me a "disgusting white colonizer," and accused me of being on the payroll of the quarry company.

After the meeting I wrote her a letter and suggested that since she'd never met me before, if we were to have a frank exchange of ideas she might find me less disgusting. She replied that she still thought I was disgusting and that pretty much ended the dialogue. I also have a letter in my desk that reads, in part, "I've completely lost all respect for you as an elected official and as a human being." I like to keep that letter close, just in case my ego goes completely out of control. Other than deaths and illness, it was, literally, the worst time in my life.

I'm sure Sol Alinsky and his "Rules for Radicals" have done a lot of good in the world, but there are times when those rules are misapplied. For instance, one of the rules suggests that the best way to unite an organization is to find a common enemy that can be demonized. When you're operating in a small place, quite often the govern-

ment officials you're demonizing over one issue are the
same people who are on your church council and coach-
ing the youth basketball team, plus they're the people you
need to go to for funding parks and building a free mental
health clinic. Newt Gingrich did much the same thing in
1990 when he sent out a pamphlet advising Republican
candidates to use the terms sick, radical, and traitor to
describe Democrats. The reason Sol and Newt advocated
these strategies is because they work. By and large, they are
a perfect prescription for short term, immediate gains.

Sadly, they are also catastrophic for the full integration
of a community and society for larger goals because while
"us against them, the bastards," works for football teams
the continuous splintering into smaller and smaller groups
works against the best interests of society as a whole.

I'm willing to believe that folks on the far left and far
right are serious and sincere in their beliefs, the same way
I'm willing to believe that Welsh is a language and jazz is an
art form and not random noises slapped in place as long-
running practical jokes, but this doesn't mean I understand
the first thing about either flank.

Over the past few years I've tried not to let my hurt
feelings at the personal attacks on my integrity affect my
work, but it isn't easy. I think of myself as a good guy, and I
work at it. One of my fondest memories is of a woman who
had ridden the school bus as an elementary student when I
was a senior. When she met one of my granddaughters she
told her, "When I was your age, your papa was the big kid
who protected me." I loved that; it might be the nicest thing
anyone has ever said about me.

The zoning issue, combined with the uproar over my
café project did huge damage to my self-image. It was hard
finding out that I was not, in fact, a good guy. It reminded
me of the time I thought I was channeling Shane only to

be presented with photographic evidence that I was not Shane, I was a chubby kid with a limp blonde crew cut, wearing a ketchup stained t-shirt and sitting bareback on a Welsh pony named Kelly.

Oh, well. After giving it some more thought, I'd have to say my opinion is that the application of Alinsky's "Rules for Radicals" by both ends of the political spectrum has probably done more damage to society than it has good.

It was a cold March morning when I turned on the lights and finally flipped the "Closed" sign to open for the first time in three years.

About an hour later, Dougie came in and asked if I was making breakfast. He had noticed the sign. To this date that's still the only advertising I've ever done.

Years earlier, Dougie may have pronounced what might well be my epitaph. He's a carpenter, and I was helping him install some sheetrock in our basement. I was chattering away about something that I'd found interesting when I noticed that I wasn't hearing the sound of his screw gun. I turned and saw him looking at me with a look of not completely approving fascination. He said, "Brent, you know more shit that don't matter than anyone I know."

March and April were a little slow at the café, which was fine, as I was still learning how to cook. I need to offer a retroactive apology to anyone who ordered scrambled eggs the first few months. I'd cook them on the grill and it would take about twenty seconds before I could slap a yellowish-green hockey puck on a plate.

Business picked up in June when the snowbirds returned from Arizona and Texas, and things got really busy later in the summer when there was the 130th celebration of the Founding of Clinton. That was the day we discovered that one of my sisters, a woman who had a 4.0 in her Masters of Nursing course and has exhibited stunning competence in almost every aspect of her life, is perhaps the worst waitress in all of Christendom—a surprise to all of us. At one point when we had perhaps forty people waiting for food she came into the kitchen and said, "I can't believe I'm so bad at this!"

No, Myrlah, I couldn't believe it either.

It was about that time a young woman wandered into the café looking for a job as a waitress. I didn't really want a waitress, but I was yearning for a cook so that I could have an occasional day off. Since this was the first time since 1975 that I was forced to be in the same place at the same time every day, I was feeling a little stifled. I do understand that there are people, many good, decent people, who have to show up at the same time and the same place for days in a row. I've just never been one of them before.

I figured if she was willing to work as a waitress I could teach her how to cook.

Turns out I was wrong.

Doing all the work myself I could break even with eight customers a day—that's if I worked for free. With a paid waitress I needed eighteen, which meant I lost money nine out of every ten days. I started encouraging Kayla to go to college and even considered starting up a scholarship for her, just to get her to leave.

I still never got a day off, because the one time I left Kayla in charge a woman left the café muttering, "I'm never coming back again if that girl is cooking."

Someone told me about the comment so I sent her a re-fund, along with a nice note encouraging her to try us one more time. She still hasn't come back. In a town with only four hundred people I couldn't afford too many customers like her.

As the months passed I needed my alarm less and less. I'd finally resolved my omelet issues. When things slowed down I'd plug in my laptop, wipe the bacon grease off my hands and try to get a little writing done. Kayla finally did leave for school. Even though it meant I was working much harder, it was a vast relief the day I gave her a hundred dollar bonus and a small hug and sent her on her way.

A common question at this point might be, "What the hell were you thinking?"

Let me explain.

Lesson 1
Rescue the Kitten

Almost four years ago, I was 5,327 words into a project that I was hoping would come in at around 36,000 when my email alert dinged.

First was a message from a guy who runs a school in the mountains of Haiti high above Jacmel. He was wondering if I could write a press release for his project. The second message was from a county employee reminding me that I had agreed to spend four evenings teaching "Love and Logic" parental discipline classes, which I'd become involved in because I'd seen far too many reports cross my desk concerning the end result of what happens when children grow up unloved and undisciplined.

Suddenly the messages were coming fast and furious. Amy Klobuchar and Al Franken needed money to fight off the ravening hordes of Republicans, I had homework for an Arts Council Visioning Session, and someone I'd never met wanted me to sign a book and mail it to her. Someone else I'd never met wanted to yell at me about my role on a Planning and Zoning Commission that's studying the license application for a new quarry—a brand new economic development project in a place that goes decades without one—and as a county commissioner I feel stuck between protecting pristine, three billion year old granite outcroppings and making sure that old people have food, and child-abusers are locked up.

Another message was from my father, wondering if I could go with him to an estate-planning workshop. His goals are to take care of my mom, to die before Alzheimer's kicks in, and to have the farm stay in the family without any fights among siblings after he's gone. The seminar is six hours long, plus six hours of driving to get there and back. I'm not sure it can answer all his questions, but it seems worth the time.

I did some consultation about tile choices for a kitchen—not mine, the one in my hometown restaurant that some folks were rehabbing in hopes of getting a tenant. I'd agreed to lay the tile floor, but there was still spirited debate about sink placement.

The last message in the scrum concerned a Board of Ordained Ministry retreat I was scheduled to attend, which involves the Minnesota United Methodist Church scrutinizing people who've spent at least a decade, and in some cases their entire lives, preparing for ministry, then deciding whose heart to break.

I took a deep breath, leaned back in my chair, rubbed my scarred, bald head, and said to myself, "I just want to write. Why can't these people leave me alone so I can get back to my real life?"

My own, internal message alert dinged, and the message I was receiving read, "Maybe this is your real life."

Maybe it is. Maybe even though I think I have several good novels, another collection of essays and perhaps a movie locked inside me, none of that will happen.

I've taken several Meyers-Briggs tests in my life, and for the past decade I've been classified as an INFJ. That means, if I may condense, that I don't enjoy being in charge of things, but I really hate seeing things done badly. And anyone who has spent as much time as I have involved in local government and church affairs has seen more stuff done badly than any one life should allow.

I could blame the cat for this, but really, it wasn't the cat's fault. No matter how you cut it, I'm the one who has to take responsibility.

Let me explain. My first years were spent in a very small house. It had a few tiny rooms, no bathroom, a cement block basement, and a badly made patch in the ceiling above the sink courtesy of my father when he stepped through the drywall while insulating the attic. The house sat inside the shelter of a grove, two hundred feet from my paternal grandparent's house, on a tiny plot of land my father bought from his father shortly before he was married.

The front steps were poured concrete with a sand interior, but the sand hadn't been compacted properly and had settled away, providing a haven for garter snakes that basked on the top step on sunny spring days. Sixty years later the garter snakes still thrive, though the house has been gone for nearly fifty years.

In the basement, a large galvanized tub captured rainwater from the eaves troughs. I think my mom used that soft water to wash clothes, in an effort to keep iron stains from the well water from ruining clothes they couldn't afford to replace.

When I was around three, I remember walking past the basement window and hearing a kitten cry. It caught my ear, but I was on a mission of some sort and didn't bend over to look through the cobwebbed window into the dark and dank room.

The next day, my mother found a drowned kitten that had stumbled and fallen into the tub. I could have saved it, but I didn't know that and I didn't take the time.

I've never missed a bus. I've never been late for a plane or lost in a subway. I barely sleep at night—this time of month as the moon moves towards full is the worst, the slightest sound in the night makes my eyes pop open. The monitoring equipment for my sleep apnea test showed that instead of waking when my blood oxygen levels dropped by 10% or so, as is usual, I stirred toward wakefulness when they dropped as little as 3%.

The doctor used the word "hyper-vigilance" to describe my reactions. I don't know if he invented the word or not. I do know my children tease me about living my life in "Worst Case Scenario World."

I should have looked in that basement window. It wouldn't have taken that long. I was only three, it's not like I was late for work. The drowned kitten isn't my first memory—that's standing at the screen door watching my older sisters get on the school bus—but it is the most vivid memory of my early childhood. I was walking on the west side of the house, near a patch of hollyhocks. I heard a noise, glanced to my left and found that I was next to the tiny, cobwebbed window that accessed the basement. I knew the sound was a kitten in some sort of distress, but my curiosity did not extend to retracing my steps and going into the basement to investigate.

"Agile as a cat" is an axiom that doesn't really resonate with me. I've watched cats do incredibly clumsy things— emptying bookshelves in passing, falling off of fences, and lurching from one side of the driveway to the other without actually getting out of the way of an oncoming vehicle. It's so easy to visualize the kitten climbing up on the rim, sniffing curiously and tumbling in.

Just last week, I spent two hours with a bottle of Dawn dish detergent and a five gallon pail full of warm water, scrubbing used motor oil off of four kittens who had, one after another, fallen into the pan I'd put under the drain when I'd changed the oil in my pickup. One I can understand, but all four?

The galvanized tub in my parent's basement was only about half full of water. Completely full or completely empty would have been okay, but the rule about never seeing a skeleton of a cat up a tree does not apply to metal tubs with tall, straight, un-clawable and un-leapable sides.

If I didn't have a vivid imagination, I know I'd have to be looking for a real job, but it is not an unmixed blessing. My sleep is often restless and troubled, and the kitten has played a role in many nightmares over the years. In fact, my dreams have become something of a barometer—when the struggling kitten makes a nighttime appearance, there's something in my life that my subconscious says requires attention.

I didn't tell anyone then, and several decades passed before I told anyone at all. A small farm on the edge of the prairie in the late Fifties, where everyone was working as hard as they could just to keep up, did not highly value the life of a stray kitten. I imagine my sisters shed a few tears and my parents felt badly for a few minutes. As for me, I watched it all carefully and didn't say a word.

If that experience was my worry vaccination, I received my booster shot a few years later. About the time I hit double digits in age, I talked my parents into getting me a horse. He was a crossbreed, Welsh pony with something else, with a dark mane and tail, an inelegant head and the non-poetic name of "Kelly."

About the same time, I'd found an old book titled "The Lance of Kanana." It filled my head with images of noble Arabian steeds, at least when I wasn't busy imagining myself as Shane, the hero of the best Western ever written. To an outside eye, Kelly might not have seemed like an appropriate sidekick for fantasies, but I've always been a fan of rejecting reality. That same outside eye also might have concluded that a chubby blonde boy with a limp crew-cut, baggy blue jeans and a stained white t-shirt wasn't all that likely as hero material. Kelly and I had several good years chasing outlaws or infidels, depending on the day.

As I moved into my teen years, heroic fantasies became less important than … well … girls. And, the horse became less important, too.

One day I wandered out to untether him and move him from one patch of grass to another. He jerked at the rope when I untied it. I never knew whether he was impatient to move, thirsty because I hadn't watered him, or just feeling grumpy. The lead rope slipped from my hands and Kelly bolted away, the way horses sometimes do, from a dead stop to a panic-stricken gallop, with the panic building its own momentum until the horse didn't even know why it was running. The gallop ended when Kelly burst through a gate and broke his right rear leg nearly off at the hock. I can still see it dangling down, raw and bloody, like a dislocated chicken leg right before the last cut with the knife. My dad called a neighbor who owned a deer rifle, my mom ushered me to the house, and I no longer needed to worry about horse chores.

It would have been so easy.

If I'd just saved the kitten, watered the horse on time, and not dropped the lead rope, perhaps now I wouldn't be spending too much time in meetings and on the road, feeling a vague anxiety that everything bad that happens in the world is somehow my fault.

I've been under general anesthesia half a dozen times in my life. Truthfully, I'm starting to lose track of how many things have needed fixing—hiatal hernia, gall bladder, appendix, double hernia, as well as random collisions with pointy objects. If you play connect-the-dots with the scars on my torso, you end up with something that looks a little like the map of Florida. If you include the scars from the knee operation, there's even a spot for Key West.

Those moments laying crucified on an operating table, right before I drift into unconsciousness, are perhaps the only times in my life when I'm truly relaxed. There's always the chance that this time I won't wake up, and it won't be my fault. I wonder how many suicides are averted just by pride, by the fervent desire not to have "Well, that was stupid" as the subtext of the eulogy. But to just fall asleep? It wouldn't be as good as rescuing a child from a burning building, but still, it wouldn't be a bad way to go out. I wonder if my grandchildren know that looking out for them saves me just as much as it saves them.

Saving the cat all those years ago wouldn't have been for only my benefit. Show some mercy for my family and colleagues. They deal with this grumpy guy who feels that if everyone just paid attention and stopped screwing around, we could take care of the children and old folks, protect the environment, and perhaps turn back time to undo the ravages of colonialism.

That last one is a little iffy, but I'm working on it.

Lesson 2
Know Who You Were

One of my favorite topics to speak about is "Who we are is who we were." I believe that. There are some self-made folks out there but, for most of us, our family and the old folks around us when we were kids determine, to a large extent, the people we become.

Before you get too invested in this book, take a few minutes and read about some of the people who made me who I am.

Mom

We might as well start with my mother. She grew up on a succession of small farms in western Minnesota. A succession because she grew up during the Depression and her family kept getting starved out or bankrupted. Her father spent quite a bit of his spare time organizing his fellow farmers and was a leader in the Farmer's Union movement. He was small, and Welsh, and smoked Winston cigarettes. On Christmas Eve he would stop for a holiday drink on his way home from work, and my grandmother would wring her hands in despair with the certainty that his backsliding would mean he was going to hell and she was doomed to spend eternity without him. Grandma was a good Methodist, and a member of the Women's Christian Temperance Union. I'm not certain that made her easy to live with.

However, there were indications that I may have missed some of the finer nuances of her character.

When I was a freshman in college a buddy and I spent the better part of a month roaming the county where I grew up, doing an independent study on … I'm not sure what, I just knew a professor gave us permission to not be in class for a month. As part of the project we spent a day in conversation with my grandmother and some of her buddies. They talked with glee about a nickel auction back in the Dirty Thirties.

For those of you unfamiliar with Depression-era Midwestern farm lore, every now and then, when banks were foreclosing right and left, when a farm auction was scheduled, a group of farmers would get together, intimidate the other potential purchasers into silence, then buy all the farmer's possessions for a nickel and return the farm to him. After that, he could start over, free and clear.

My grandmother told the story of how her husband and some of his friends had pulled off a few of these somewhat questionable transactions, and when the next one was scheduled the banker arranged for the sheriff to be in attendance. Shortly before the auction began, the sheriff was lured into a corncrib where he was stripped to his long johns and locked up for the duration. The old ladies cackled with glee at the memory, and I remember thinking that perhaps her Methodism could occasionally be ousted by a darker and older religion.

I never knew much about the ancestry on that side of the family, although they were my most interesting relatives. Holidays with my dad's side of the family involved good food, quiet discussions of the weather and crops and a certain amount of softball. On my mom's side there were political disputes, an uncle with an awe-inspiring talent for profanity, and a certain number of unplanned pregnancies and other irregularities. I didn't know much more about them until our oldest daughter went on a college choir trip to Wales and spent an evening in a bar with the members of a men's choir. She was the youngest person in the room by approximately five decades and when they found out her grandmother's maiden name the men were entranced.

One said, "You can always tell a Griffith, but you can't tell them much." That brought gales of laughter and a few nods of agreement. Another old man said reassuringly, "The thing about the Griffiths is, their hearts are as big as their mouths." That's not a lot of info for a quarter of my heritage, even though it seems accurate.

As the oldest child on a small farm where there was always more work to be done then time to do it, my mom spent her youth taking care of her younger brother and sisters. This meant getting them to sit on the ground while she stood over them with a schoolbook and a lesson plan.

You see, my mother is a teacher.

Not an "I'll take some education classes so I have a fallback plan" and not an "I'll be a teacher so I'll have summers off" teacher, but a teacher. It was a career she was born for, and she knew it from her earliest days.

She graduated from high school in 1942, had six months of teacher training and started her career in a succession of country schools. First was District 12 in Malta

Township, where she was smaller than most of her students and only a couple years older than some of them. From there she went to District 63 in Big Stone Township, followed by District 10 back in Malta Township. One of her students was a little girl who came to school very excited one day because her big brother was coming home from the war and might pick her up after school. He did, and that was the end of her teaching career, for a few years.

She was a stay at home mom for three kids, at least for a while. To supplement the income generated by a small farm in the Fifties (which was roughly zero) she raised chickens and sold eggs.

Now in her nineties, she has a very bad back—in pain on her good days, immobile on her bad.

I was young during her chicken-raising days, but I have a clear memory of buckets of water going one way and buckets of eggs coming the other. She used her egg money to buy groceries and pay for piano lessons for my sisters.

It's funny the connections a mind makes. Whenever I think about my mom collecting eggs I think of the old labor union song "Bread and Roses." First written sometime before World War I, it is a plea by female mill workers for enough wages and security so they could buy food, but also so they could live whole lives. I think of those smelly chickens, tended by a woman who knew she was born to be a teacher. She used those eggs to buy sustenance and culture, our bread and roses.

But not for long. I was the baby of the family, so when I was safely in the school system, she went back to school herself. This was in the early Sixties, when such a notion was radical indeed. She was in her thirties, and an old woman on the University of Minnesota, Morris campus. She was a dreaded curve wrecker in her classes—not interested in football games or extracurricular activities, instead going to class, sitting in front and taking notes with a look of grim determination.

Her college attendance took all the family's spare money and all her time. We lived on TV dinners and Tater Tot Hot Dish.

Perhaps the angriest I ever saw my father was when my mother was taking summer school courses and he and I were batching it. I was about twelve at the time and spent most of my time reading science fiction and ducking farm chores. One day he popped his head in the house about 3:00 p.m. He rattled off a series of instructions, something along the lines of, "Start the oven at 5:00, put a couple potatoes in, then brown some pork chops and ... do something else, followed by a nice salad."

That isn't really what he said. I can't tell you what he said, because I was twelve years old so I didn't really hear anything an adult said to me, and by the time it dawned on me that this was important I was too panicked to ask him to repeat any of it. I made a couple of TV dinners instead, like usual, and when he came in the house around 7:00 p.m. instead of a quality homemade meal there was a Salisbury steak, green beans and a potato-like substance in a tin foil tray.

I'm now older than my father was that afternoon when he dreamed of a real meal. With the benefit of considerable hindsight, I can now visualize just what a devastating blow that TV dinner was.

It's never pleasant, watching a man's dreams crushed.

It got to be a long summer, for everyone, because I never did learn how to cook. It paid off in the end, as education is supposed to do. Mom graduated from college and spent the next couple of decades as a Special Ed teacher, which honed her attraction and concern for the last and the least.

The money problem eased a little. The farm was larger and more profitable, and there was that teacher's salary so my father did some extensive remodeling to the house. Nothing spectacular—just an addition slapped on the side of an old farmhouse by a pretty fair scrub carpenter, but it meant a small nook for an office, a bathroom just for mom, and a slightly larger nook to serve as a dining room. For the dining room my mom bought an octagonal table.

She basked in the glory of what was, to her eyes, a lovely formal dining room. She actually only basked until a visit by a relative of a relative, a snooty woman who I'm proud to say I disliked from the moment I first met her. My mother was excitedly giving a tour of the new renovations and when the woman spied the table set in its little nook she said, "Why, what a lovely game table."

That was over forty years ago, but I still remember the look on my mother's face as she looked with fresh eyes and saw an ugly old farmhouse downwind of a hog barn, with a cheap table stuck in a small corner of a paneled room. Mercifully the woman soon left. After she was gone, out of nowhere, my mom said through gritted teeth, "But dammit, I can teach naughty little boys how to read."

And she could.

Dad

My dad does things.

It's not a very long resume, but since my dad has never worked for anyone else (other than a couple years for Uncle Sam, who didn't require much of an application form as he was hiring at the time), a lack of a detailed resume has never been a huge hindrance in his career.

Actually, now that I think of it, I've hired quite a few people in my life, and if any of them had the wit to make that the first line on their resume, I would have snapped them up. We have plenty of people on this planet who plan, strategize, facilitate and orientate. There are people who can prioritize, network and conceptualize. What we have a serious lack of is people who get things done.

My father's talent is not an unmixed blessing. Along with the gift of getting things done comes a certain insensitivity to input from others, and a mild inability to see that other people might have a different set of priorities.

> We have a serious lack of people who get things done.

Strike that. No sense in being subtle here. When my dad decides something needs to be done, it becomes an immediate priority for the entire rest of the world, or at least whatever portion of it responds to his voice. (Please reference TV dinner story in the previous chapter.) I cannot count, literally, the times he's called me up, asked for my assistance on a project anytime in the next half hour, and then when I show up on his doorstep twenty minutes later he's already finished what he asked for help with. Over the past few decades I've developed the habit of dashing out the door and leaping into the pickup whenever he calls. It's just the simplest thing to do, although occasionally it's a little hard on my own schedule.

My father and I have managed a half-century or so without having a serious chat about religion. He's not much for philosophy or metaphysics, or actually any sort of speculative conversation.

About thirty years ago I had just finished reading Stephen King's "The Dead Zone", which is a book about a guy who can foresee the future and has to decide whether or not to kill a popular politician who will someday become a very bad man indeed. He was willing to trade his life for a better future for mankind, but balked at the idea of going down in history as just a dangerous nut. I found the premise fascinating and tried to start a conversation about whether or not someone could have killed Hitler in 1930. I was a third of the way into the story and hadn't even begun to elaborate on all the psychological nuances when my father interrupted me with a gruff, "Shoot the son of a bitch."

And, he probably would have, and he wouldn't have bothered to explain why he did it.

I don't really know just why he's always been so involved in a church. It's something my family has always done, at least for the past hundred years or so. As Methodists we have John Wesley's clear instructions about doing good, plus he's been a Mason for sixty years or so with all the bias towards action that implies. He does have the irritating habit of thinking that we're put on this earth to make things better, and the best way to do that is to shoulder your share of the burden, and about twenty percent more.

You know the guy in a church who sings in the choir, volunteers to read scripture and gets up and witnesses during alter calls?

My dad is not that guy.

He's the guy who cleans the gutters, checks to make sure there's oil in the lawnmower, and frets about whether the windows in the parsonage are energy efficient.

He's not a comfortable man to be around, at least not for me. He has a number of good friends, although at 89 he's outlived many of them, and I'm guessing they'd be surprised by that statement. But my dominant feeling whenever I think of my father is a vague anxiety, wondering what I've screwed up lately. He's always been very focused and not particularly communicative outside the needs of the job.

I hired my first employee when I was still in my twenties and I've come to realize it was mainly so that I would have someone willing to say, "Good morning," to me when starting a day's work.

Me

I haven't always made a living by telling stories. I grew up on a farm in a small place on the edge of the prairie. I went off to a private college when I was 18 with all my possessions on the back of a motorcycle, and all the money I'd earned in 18 years in my pockets.

I ran out of money in two semesters, then switched to the University of Minnesota. I made it through the first quarter at the U. When I sat down to fill out my class schedule for the second quarter I leafed through the massive course listings and, with a sinking feeling, realized that there was really nothing there I wanted to do. I was bored with school and in love with a girl so I quit school, and got a job at Nino's Steakhouse as a janitor and dishwasher. I found that I was better at working than I was at academics.

Also, I'd discovered that I had developed an irrational dislike of academics—those sorts of people who spend their lives clustered around college campuses. I'm over that. I've evolved since then, and I now try to judge people based on who they are as individuals and take into account that their environment may be detrimental to their development as complete human beings. Why, some of my best friends are academics.

Unless, of course, they read this.

In my defense, I come from what may well be the epicenter of practical. In the world I grew up in there was a limited amount of time and energy allotted for things that didn't matter and magical thinking.

I remember being shocked at some of the conversations I heard at college. My clearest memory is a lunchtime discussion about the Symbionese Liberation Army, which had just kidnapped Patty Hearst and was issuing various demands and manifestos. I listened for a while and then said, "Yeah, looks like the revolution is coming," and got up to get rid of my dirty dishes. A young suburban woman followed me to the counter, looked both ways, and said, "Yes, I think you're right. I think these people are the beginning of the revolution. We need to be ready for when the heavy shit goes down."

> Smart people can be very stupid.

I was speechless. In retrospect, I still am. At the time I was 18 and the list of topics I knew nothing about was nearly endless. I was sheltered, naïve, and hopelessly unsophisticated. But even I knew these guys weren't the revolution—their incoherent political strategies were only overshadowed by their incompetence. Furthermore, if these guys really were the revolution, earnest young private college students would probably be the first ones against the wall. How could she not see that? That was an important moment for me, well worth the entire year's tuition all by itself.

Up until then I hadn't realized that smart people could be very stupid. That has been a very valuable insight to me. Over the years I've added to it. While there are plenty of stupid people in the world and they do cause a great deal of trouble, all the really devastating problems we're faced with have been caused or exacerbated by smart people.

The only other thing I learned at Hamline University came to me on a beautiful spring day when a sociology professor entered the classroom and said, "I really don't feel like teaching today. You all can have the day off." A Vietnam vet, recently returned to civilian life, spoke up and said, "Do you have any idea what this class is costing me? You have no right to take a day off."

I'd been anticipating an afternoon spent doing … well, doing the sort of stuff a 19 year old would do. But instead we spent the class hour discussing the vet's point of view. That was the first time I really understood that as a society we live in a net of mutual responsibility, where the actions of one can and do affect the lives of many.

Two little nuggets of insight in exchange for a year's tuition might not seem like much, but I know people who've done a lot worse in a year of college and, quite frankly, I've had entire years since then where I didn't learn that much.

What I learned in two years at Hamline and the University of Minnesota pales in comparison to what I learned in three months at Nino's Steakhouse. I learned that an old football jersey is the proper dishwashing attire because the sleeves are just short enough that you can reach into dirty water and unplug a drain without getting them wet. I learned that while I like the things you can do with money, there are things I won't do for money.

I learned that while I like feeling as if I'm part of a team, I'm always most comfortable off in a corner by myself, doing something that matters.

I lived in a cheap apartment two freeways away from where I worked. It was a ten minute commute with a car, but in the depths of winter I pulled out of the parking lot at my girlfriend's apartment building and when I turned the steering wheel there appeared to be no connection to the front wheels. I sailed across the street and gently bumped into the Honeywell building. We got it back into the parking lot by having my girlfriend drive while I ran alongside and kicked the wheels in the direction I wanted to go.

This development changed my morning routine.

I left for work about 5:00 a.m., caught a bus to downtown Minneapolis, transferred to the bus that took me to the West Bank of the U, caught the Intercampus bus to

Saint Paul and then hitchhiked the last two miles, getting
to work around 8:00 a.m. If I caught a ride right away I'd
be fifteen minutes early for work and would have to stand
around in the doorway shivering until the assistant manager showed up to unlock the door.

The shop said I needed several hundred dollars in parts
to properly fix the car, a sum beyond all measure. After a
few days hitchhiking I spent a Saturday afternoon on my
back on the frozen pavement of a parking lot, figuring
out the problem. There was a tiny spring-loaded ball and
socket joint that had come apart. I realize that any responsible mechanic would replace the entire joint, but I put
four pennies behind the worn out spring and pounded the
joint back together. As an added safety measure I wrapped
a wire clothes hanger around the whole thing. My repair
held up for several years, until a bad winter and a poor
choice of parking spots buried the car under fifteen feet of
snow, caving in the roof and breaking the windows.

I always thought that was a fortunate breakdown for
me, in terms of a learning experience. Ever since that
winter when someone starts speaking knowledgably about
lazy black people my mind's eye flips back 40 years to that
5:00 a.m. bus stop where all the other faces shivering in
the morning cold were black. Years later I read "Travels
with Charley" and laughed out loud when I read how John
Steinbeck had a similar experience. He knew only one
black family growing up, outstanding individuals from
top to bottom, and when someone would ask, "Would you
want your sister to marry one?" he would think, "They
might not think my sister was good enough."

My wife and I were married in 1975, two years to the
day after our first date. With extreme diligence, and living
on a diet of peanut butter sandwiches and five-cans-for-a-
dollar tomato soup, we had managed to save a little over

$2,000. We spent a few hundred on the wedding and the rest on six weeks in Europe.

Travel is supposed to be a broadening experience. Seeing Michelangelo's David was certainly life changing, plus we ran into a wonderful man in Lugano, Switzerland who took us to a youth hostel when we were lost in the rain. We found out that storekeepers in Geneva treat young, broke travelers as if they were young and broke.

Also, evading customs and immigration in Ireland carries no real penalty. Plus, when camped on the beach, giant snails will climb your tent and be ominous black blobs to be seen upon awaking.

I'm sure there was more that I learned, but those are the lessons that come to mind.

When we came home we moved into an abandoned house a mile and a half from my folks. The previous occupant was my Norwegian bachelor Great-Uncle Carl. Before him there were just my great-grandparents who'd built the house. That summer we felt their ghosts all around us, along with occasionally hearing their footsteps upstairs.

Hearing the ghosts that summer didn't really bother us so much—after all, they were all family and it would be hard for me to believe they would have malevolent intent. They might not have been comfortable to be around—my Uncle Carl was famous for saying, to any of the several teenage boys who spent summers working for him, "You gotta OBSERVE, boy!" but it was always said with the intent to educate, not to torment.

This phrase would come out whenever the boy did something stupid, and if you've ever spent much time around a teenage boy, you can imagine how often that phrase could be heard. I never heard it myself, because by the time I was old enough for him to consider stupidity a choice, he was no longer living near us. He struggled with what today would probably be diagnosed as severe bipolar disorder, which twice landed him in a state mental institution getting electric shock treatments. The second time, when he came out the other side of the dark, he checked himself into a nursing home a two hour's drive away from his farm. I've always thought he had to choose between farming, this job he did supremely well but that made him crazy, and sanity, and he chose the latter. I've always admired that choice—I wish more people would make it.

It's just as well Uncle Carl's ghost didn't talk to me that first summer. I had long hair and a wild beard, and I'm not sure he approved of the way the grass grew long and a tattered screen door leaned against the side of the house all summer long. We have a picture from that first summer— my new wife sitting on the battered cement steps next to the old screen door, with her bare, tanned feet curled in front of her and a wild tomcat she'd tamed on her lap.

It's funny what memory does. My recollections of that summer are almost all good. We were twenty years old and newlyweds. Eight hours of work a day used up only half the daylight, leaving plenty of spare time for doing whatever we wanted. We bought an orange Chevy Vega and paid for it in four months by baling flax straw after work.

Perhaps there are unhappier elements of that time that have escaped my memory, I say this because that summer was the second time in my life that I went to the doctor with symptoms of an ulcer, and it was the first time I had what became a series of recurring nightmares.

The stomach pain was the fault of my painfully overdeveloped sense of responsibility, which even on a good day leaves me feeling like most of the evils of the world can be laid at my door because I just don't care enough to really do what matters. In particular, that summer I worked at Orcon Industries, where we made the worst farm equipment on the planet. Truckloads of subsoilers and truck beds would leave and return a week later, rejected by equipment dealerships across the entire Midwest.

By the end of the summer I was foreman of my department—because everyone else had been laid off or fired. It was my first real experience of having authority over people, because as part of my shipping department duties I had responsibility for the paint department—two middle-aged ladies who worked with spray guns and 55-gallon barrels of orange paint. I didn't know anything about painting, or managing employees, but I'd been told I was in charge so I hovered, frantically trying to be of use. In the end one of the ladies turned to me and said, "Brent, go away. We'll call if we need you."

> If people know what they are doing, leave them alone.

"Okay," I said, and went away. It's probably the single best bit of management advice I've every internalized. If people know what they're doing, leave them alone.

I don't know if my adventures in management were what prompted the nightmares, but they have been beauties—I'm stuck in the middle of an open field and there is a monstrous tank clanking in pursuit of me, and no matter how I twist and turn it chases me until I fall to the ground and watch helplessly as the steel tracks approach my prone body. I've always woken up before I'm run over, but some nights as I lay in bed with sweat running off my face and my pulse pounding in my ears, I'm not certain that's a fair tradeoff.

In the fall of 1975 we headed off to Waseca, where I was going to go to school to learn how to be a farmer.

Those were very good years to be a farmer. The anchovies off the coast of Peru had disappeared, which meant that animal feed in America needed a protein source other than fishmeal, and soybean meal was the next best alternative. That quadrupled the price of soybeans in a matter of a few months, and for the first time since World War II there was money in farming. Before then people farmed because they couldn't do anything else, or because they loved living in the country. That was the beginning of the time when people went into farming just for the money, and those were strange and heady days indeed.

> Beware of the corporate mother-fucker.

My wife got a job manufacturing CB radios. She worked as an inspector, sitting at the end of an assembly line with a little plywood stand where she would set radios before she would inspect them for loose wires and solder lumps. Because she is smart, with good eyes and clever fingers, she soon became good at her work, to the point that she would have to sit and wait for the next radio to come down the line. To fill the time she did little wood burnings with her soldering iron—bunnies frolicking under trees for example. One day a foreman happened by and saw her handiwork. The next day they brought a new plywood stand, this one painted black so her wood burnings wouldn't show, and my wife just sat quietly and waited for her next radio.

That was another learning experience for me. I told some people about the incident and one friend of a friend nodded wisely and said, "The corporate motherfucker strikes again."

Yes he had, and he's struck many more times over the years. I've always been glad that I had a name to attribute to him, even though it's not a phrase you can drop into just any conversation.

We lived in an absolute dump. You know those little roadside motels that are tiny, individual cabins? You don't see them very often anymore; even forty years ago they were being phased out. We managed to get a winter's lease on one in an over-heated rental market where there was nothing else available anywhere close to our price range. The bathroom was across the street and we cooked in an electric frying pan we'd received for a wedding present. After supper we would fill the pan with hot water and wash our dishes in it. As fall wore on we were deluged with mice looking for a winter shelter. I'd heard someplace that mothballs keep mice away and so we soon lived in a dump with no kitchen or bathroom that reeked of mothballs.

When I tell this story, people always express their sympathy. It's not why I tell the story—I didn't think we needed sympathy then and I still don't. We were really very happy—no money, of course, but we didn't need much money. We didn't do much socializing, but we never have.

I don't remember being bored. In the spring when we packed up our furniture we discovered a few shrunken, moldy oranges—remnants of a week in January when we'd spent the long evenings learning how to juggle. Without a TV, and long before there was such of thing as the Internet, we should have been bored beyond redemption in our little hovel; the only thing I can remember is being eager to finish school and get back to the farm. I liked the accounting classes and even business law, but when I started the crops class where I was expected to identify dried weeds by their Latin names my school days were numbered. We returned to the prairie in the spring.

It was hard.

Actually, only in hindsight do I see how hard it was. My father is a wonderful man, but he's never really been … instructional. He expects knowledge to be passed on by osmosis, and if you don't learn it's because you're not paying attention. That first spring on the prairie he bought a new grain drill and told me to go plant the wheat.

I'd never planted wheat before and I didn't do a very good job. He was angry about it most of the summer. Luckily, the worst drought in a hundred years hit and all the crops in the county dried up and blew away. It was a total weather catastrophe—it didn't matter how skillfully the ground was planted, the crops all died just the same.

This established somewhat of a theme for the three decades I farmed. I was competent as a farmer, and that competence combined with my frenzied concern about providing for my family helped ensure that I always made enough money. But I was not ferociously monomaniacal in my pursuit of farming as a profession.

The upside of that is I never ended up in a state mental institution getting electroshock therapy like my great-uncle Carl. The downside is there were any number of lapses and loose endings in my farm enterprise that made my father grit his teeth in (mostly) silent frustration.

My low boredom threshold also led me into several enterprises, some of them more successful than others, and some of them spectacular failures. I purchased my father-in-law's farm in 1980. The next year the farm economy crashed, and by 1983 the land was worth half what I had paid for it. It took a decade to pay off all those bills.

I'd just barely poked my head above water when I went into the barbecue pork business and lost a quarter of a million dollars, followed quickly by being asked to join the board of an ethanol plant start-up, which created a hundred million dollars of wealth for my friends and neighbors and returned my own investment 1,500 percent.

Along the way, my wife and I put three kids through college, had four books published, filed stories from six continents, and led short-term volunteers in mission trips to places like Kingston, Jamaica.

Lesson 3
Figure Out What Matters, and What Works

My last book had the subtitle, "Figuring Out What Matters" and the cover photo was of one of my granddaughters and me walking down a gravel road. She was about two at the time, wearing a little sundress and sandals, and she's striding down the road with the teetering, confident strides that only a two year old can achieve. I'm on her right, looking down at her, poised to lunge and grab if she should happen to stumble. In a world of confusion and clutter, this is something around which I have utter clarity.

She is what matters, she and her siblings, and cousins, and second cousins, and all the other children to whom they are related only by height, age, and vulnerability. If I had a starving child to feed and the only thing to eat was the last bald eagle on earth, I'd be plucking in a matter of minutes. I might have tears streaming down my face, but I'd still be plucking.

Of course, I hope it doesn't come to that.

Now that I know, have fully established, and am at peace about the priorities in my world I have to move on to the next step. Because after you've figured out what matters, you need to figure out what works.

That's a little harder. We live in a complicated world. While there is plenty of greed and malevolence floating around and darkening the sky, we also have a vast amount of ignorance and apathy, which does just as much harm. And we also have thousands, or millions of good-hearted people working diligently with faith and commitment to accomplish … not much

> To figure out what works, take a close and clear look at what doesn't.

at all. We need to take a look at that, because to figure out what works, we need to take a close and clear look at what doesn't. That's where I come in. Because I have done it wrong. More than once.

Way more than once. For instance, in 1983 the junior high Sunday School class had lost their teacher, through no real fault of their own (other than that they were all in junior high), and they asked me if I would step in. I thought it was the sort of thing I could do so I said, "Why not? I'll take a whack at it."

That's a default answer for me, and it occasionally leads me astray.

The students were a little dispirited, what with no one wanting to be their teacher, so I regularly gave them little pep talks. One Sunday I got really revved up and said, "You know, guys, if you work hard enough and plan carefully enough, you can do anything."

A thirteen year old boy in the corner named Eric Slieter said, "I want to go to Jamaica."

"Then we'll go to Jamaica!" I said.

It was probably a couple of weeks before I even mentioned to my wife what I had agreed to do. It did seem like a long shot, but the kids didn't forget. That first group of kids showed impressive trust and an endearing ability to commit.

We settled on congregational dinners as our choice of fundraising activities, so about once a month for years we'd be in the church basement with a half-dozen kids on Saturday mornings. We joked that they might not be able to make a fried egg, but they'd all have the recipe for hot dish for one hundred committed to memory.

It took a few years and a lot of hot dish but we were finally ready to go to Jamaica.

But why go? I don't believe I ever thought to ask Eric why he wanted to go. The kids had thought that the trip to Jamaica would include some time on a beach. And the rest of the time in the ocean with perhaps a little time for shopping thrown in. I couldn't find any scriptural backing for a trip like that, so I started scrounging around looking for something a little more useful.

This was a long time ago, several decades in fact, and the mission trip system was not as fully in place then as it is now. Or maybe it was, and I just didn't know it was there. I ended up calling directory information and getting the Methodist District Headquarters in Kingston, Jamaica, and talking to whoever answered the phone. I worked my way through several puzzled Jamaicans. My Minnesota accent and complete naiveté was a barrier to them, but after a few phone calls and a couple of letters we had a task and a place to stay lined up. Then we started to look into plane tickets. When you're on a tight budget and traveling with thirteen people, every dollar you save adds up.

What we had found out was the Jamaica was incredibly cheap to get to, if you flew on a tourist charter and landed in Montego Bay. The church we were supposed to work on was near the harbor in the heart of downtown Kingston.

Kingston is kitty-corner across the country from Montego Bay, but the road map I received in the mail showed several possible routes. The one that caught my eye would take us straight from the airport on Highway A1, and then keeping the ocean on our left side, we would switch to A3, which would take us across the mountains and down into Kingston, right onto Constant Spring Road. Constant Spring Road is where the Methodist District Headquarters was located. So, a couple hundred miles of driving, with a left turn coming out of the airport and a right turn when we reached our destination. This seemed like the way to go.

Here was the problem. I'm from western Minnesota, the beginning of the Great Plains. I live on the very south end of the remains of glacial Lake Agassiz, which is a chunk of land 400 miles long and 100 wide that has the topography of the bottom of a mud puddle. The roads are laid out in squares every mile; if you pick your destination carefully you can drive for several hundred miles without turning your steering wheel more than a quarter of a turn and never hit a curve that makes you slow down. If you take a left at Fargo you can travel another thousand miles before anything significant gets in your way.

This is different than the road from Montego Bay to Kingston. I'm sure I was aware of that, but what I probably thought was, "It's only a hundred miles. How bad can it be?" This was pre-Google Maps, long before MapQuest. If today I would have checked the route and seen it was around a hundred miles with a driving time of over four hours, I might have given some thought as to just how bad the road might be.

Turns out it can be really bad. We landed in Montego Bay and went to claim our rental van. We had a half-dozen teenagers, our three kids (the youngest being three), and our mother-in-law who was there for moral support and free childcare.

At that time, in my part of the country, cultural diversity was when the Swedish Lutherans would agree to attend Lenten services at the Norwegian Lutheran church. One of the girls on our trip had never seen a black person in the flesh until we landed in Jamaica. We left a Minnesota winter. When the plane circled Montego Bay our young people cheered as they looked out the windows and saw the changing hues of Caribbean blue water dotted with sailboats and windsurfers. We cruised down a runway dotted with the dismembered corpses of drug smuggling planes and stopped next to some palm trees.

We were madly out of our element. When I returned with the rental van, I found our little group huddled on the sidewalk with the luggage in the middle, looking besieged. They were surrounded by what might be called a horde of peddlers. We live in a fairly structured part of the world, where almost every social interaction could be described as subdued. It was a learning experience to be dropped into a place where much of the economic activity, from taxis to drug sales, is considerably more exuberant.

We loaded up and I pulled out of the parking lot, driving carefully on the left side of the road. The van was a stick shift so it was a little tricky changing gears left-handed. I soon mastered that, but the entire time we were on the island I never used the turn signal without first washing the windows, and I never had a conversation with anyone while I was driving because I was continually muttering to myself, "Stay on the left, stay on the left."

I was soon in a state of shock. The road was narrow, busy, and marked every mile or so by the burned corpse of a wrecked car. No doubt most of them having once been driven by sunburned tourists from the Midwest. About twenty miles out of Montego Bay I worked up the nerve to pass another car. The teenagers cheered madly. My ego soared, but while I was passing another car passed me, throwing up a shower of dirt and stones as it accelerated, half in the ditch and half on my rearview mirror.

After a couple of hours I stopped and bought some street food. Jamaican cuisine had not yet penetrated Big Stone County, and when the strange smells filled the van everyone but me declined to eat. I didn't mind—I really just wanted a chance to take a deep breath and spend a little time regretting every action in my life that had led me to this place.

To make a long story short, we came down out of the mountains into Kingston long after dark. I had sweat running in a steady stream down the small of my back and everyone from the middle of the van on back was carsick. Once we left the ocean and turned inland into the mountains the whole trip had been like a rollercoaster ride, except with donkeys and overloaded sugar cane trucks.

In Kingston half the streetlights were burned out and two thirds of the street signs were missing. Between hurricanes and political unrest, marking the roads for incompetent travelers seemed not to be a priority. With the team behind me varying between catatonic and rebellious, I finally gave up and stopped at the only open gas station we'd seen in three hours. The guy behind the counter had never heard of the Deaconess House, but the lady behind me in line, an IBM salesperson and dedicated Methodist, had. She gave me directions to a large, unmarked white house we'd driven by three times.

After that, the day got a little better, because Sister Julie answered my knock. She was a little grumpy, because she had expected us three hours earlier, but when I explained the route I'd cleverly followed her mouth dropped open, and she looked as if she couldn't decide whether to laugh or cry.

I knew the feeling.

Lesson 4
Work Yourself Out of the Job

Sister Julia was born in 1923 in Kingston, Jamaica. In 1954, she began the process of becoming a Deaconess. She was ordained in 1960. Other than a year spent studying and speaking in England, she spent the next thirty years working in Jamaica, the bulk of the time trying to nurture the bodies and save the souls of the poorest people.

And they are some very poor people indeed. This was my first experience with poverty in the developing world, or actually any poverty at all. I grew up on a small farm on the edge of the prairie and I didn't know anyone really poor, just as I didn't know anyone really rich. No one I knew had much money. Some had less than others—there were kids who came to school in the same clothes more often than not, and there were kids who ate as much as possible at noon lunch. Hungry babies in tattered clothes, narrow alleys lined with watchful eyes, and the knowledge that there was no way I was going to blend in anywhere … that was all new.

I've learned a lot since then. That first trip is a few decades behind me. As I write this I'm 61 years old. In the past decade I've filed articles from six continents. I've been on a half-dozen overseas work projects, and I've been on a dozen different economic development and church mission boards. I don't know everything, but I think I have a handle on what I don't know.

People fight all the time about how much and what kinds of aid to give developing countries. That's because it's complicated, and anyone who pretends otherwise isn't paying attention. Bad governments, the sad residue of colonialism, rapacious corporations stealing resources, no education, weak families, corruption, drug wars, environmental issues … I could list another half-dozen reasons. To really fix things you need to fix all of it more or less at once. And given the stunning effectiveness of the Law of Unintended Consequences it's still easy to end up doing more harm than good.

Sister Julia was a sincerely good woman, but I'm guessing she found us profoundly irritating. She was willing to put up with us, because she wanted very much to get resources to pump into the neighborhood. No matter what you think of the root causes of poverty, it takes some money to turn the situation around. Money alone won't do it. In fact, throwing money at the problems of poverty doesn't do very much at all, but nothing happens without some resources, and that means money.

So, while a group of American teenagers escorted by some inept do-gooder adults might have been a prescription for a migraine, we also meant money. If I remember correctly, we paid a fee for room and board, an amount cheap by our standards, but pretty profitable for a dormi-

tory situation in a developing country, and then we had
to contribute a thousand dollars or more for "supplies."
Since all we did while we were there was use up about five
gallons of paint, it didn't take much to fund our purchases.
That left her a pretty good chunk to use for real work.

 Short-term volunteers are much better known these
days, but thirty years ago the concept was a little more
unusual. It's actually a wonderful idea, except when it's a
terrible one.

The theory is that a group of Americans go to a place
that really needs something. They do some work while
they're there, make friends with the locals, get a better
understanding of what a complicated world we live in, and
return home better people who've made a big difference in
a needy world.

Of course, what often happens is that you get a group
of people who see this as a chance to make themselves feel
good about leaving Minnesota or Wisconsin or Michigan
in January and going to a place like Jamaica. And these
groups are not typically loaded down with plumbers,
electricians and journeyman carpenters. Instead you get
a certain number of retired teachers and preachers, along
with teenagers with no discernible skills.

Plus, of course, you're sending people to work in a
country where quite often the most dire need is for jobs. It
could easily cost a thousand dollars a head to send some
retirees to Jamaica to work on a church project, when the
average yearly salary for a Jamaican is $2,500 a year. So, a
week's work at a community center carrying cinder blocks
by a retired fifth grade teacher doesn't make much sense
when, if she'd just sent a check they could have hired a
skilled Jamaican laborer for five months.

What makes this *sometimes* work is a simple equation—you don't care about people you don't know. That's

it. That's the only redemptive part of the whole equation. There's a reason why aid organizations put up pictures of adorable orphans instead of charts and graphs showing their financial needs. If that same fifth grade teacher hefts her cinder blocks, sits in the shade during her break and teaches little kids how to read, and then goes home and talks her church, knitting club or bowling team into sponsoring a school, which is periodically visited by the people who provide the funding in order to make sure that the funds are still being spent on the children, then we have a win-win. If the teenager who came along because it got him out of school for a week forms an attachment with his counterparts and goes home and does a presentation on the residual effect of colonialism, even if he does get most of his information straight from Wikipedia, the result is another win.

Of course, that doesn't happen all that often. We went back to Jamaica four different times over the next decade before we handed the youth group reins to a different set of adults, because our children were growing up and our bank accounts were depleted. We got better at not doing stupid stuff, but that first trip … oh my Lord. Typically Methodists don't go in for sainthood, but if we did, I'd nominate Sister Julia simply for enduring our naiveté.

Kingston in the mid-eighties was quite a place. Bob Marley was dead, but Peter Tosh was still alive. From where we were staying we could hear live music from four different bars in four different directions. The place hummed with energy and the traffic cops carried automatic weapons. Two of the major aluminum manufacturers had closed up shop, and the rising murder rate had curtailed tourism.

The jerk chicken though … that was fantastic.

We were to work at Wesley Methodist Church on Tower Street. With Sister Julia riding shotgun, we'd cram into the van and leave the sanctuary of Constant Spring Road, driving through crowded streets past the National Hero's Park—at that time a dusty, garbage strewn field—past Trench Town, and down toward the harbor.

I was very impressed when I first saw Wesley Church. It sat in the middle of a walled compound, with a new two-story community center on the far side of the lot. An old folk's home wasn't really part of the property, but it was adjacent and still within the fence. Plus, it was pretty beat up so I spent my time there doing small carpentry jobs.

It was a beautiful, huge, old church, fallen on hard times. It used to have a congregation of 2,000, which had shrunk to about 100 by the time we visited. It kept shrinking. The last time I checked, the church was closed and they were trying to start a fundraising campaign to refurbish it, again. Located in a poor part of town, the plan back in the Eighties was to spruce up the church, build a community center next to it, and use it as an anchor to revitalize the entire area.

That works, sometimes, but not all that often. Here's where development projects go south, so often. You do need an anchor, a location to build around. You also need commitment from the folks in the neighborhood. You need a certain amount of money, you need people with jobs, you need a population that is educated and motivated and you need a government that even if it isn't helping, at least isn't standing in the way.

And, you need them all more or less simultaneously.

It's really hard.

We shouldn't be surprised by that—since WWII there have been uncounted billions of dollars, and francs and pounds and kroner, spent to lift people out of poverty and it hasn't paid off nearly as well as it should have. Still, we don't give up. Fairly regularly I'll read a report or a news article about some initiative—be it micro-lending or empowering women or enhancing infrastructure—that is touted as transformative.

It never is. And there's a reason why those good ideas are so seldom replicable. A long time teacher once explained the various enthusiasms that sweep the educational world. Someone will come up with a new way to teach—a technique or a philosophy that shows remarkable promise. People jump on board, whether it is Common Core or New Math, but when it is implemented nationwide the miracle results fade away. What the teacher told me is that it isn't the particular technique or philosophy that is transformative, but the enthusiasm and commitment of the innovators who bring it to fruition. And that's what makes successes of all kinds so difficult to replicate. Techniques are easy—commitment, enthusiasm, and persistence are a lot trickier.

Sister Julia wanted to save her community, and in our ham-handed, fumbling way, we wanted to help her. I don't think we did. We'd show up, splash some paint on a wall that had been covered with graffiti the previous day. A sprinkling of folks from the neighborhood would gather to watch us work, but we were too stupid to make any sort of real connection.

I remember the first day. The teenagers wanted cold drinks and I asked a local woman if there was any place to buy food nearby. She directed me a block to the south, two blocks west. I walked there slowly, my mind churning with thoughts about what I should be doing the rest of the week. I went through the door of the tiny grocery. There was a bulletproof window across the width of the entire store, with a small grated door in the middle. People passed their money into a slot and received their groceries

> Techniques are easy. Commitment, enthusiasm, and persistence are a lot trickier.

through the grate. The pervasive smell of marijuana filled the air, and a small crowd of men who clearly had nothing better to do watched me.

It wasn't until I saw the bulletproof glass that it really came home to me how poor and volatile a place I was in. I come from a place where not only are most doors unlocked, most people don't even know where their house keys are. I'd never been in a bank that had a guard, or even a security camera. Bulletproof glass and barred windows in a grocery store were completely beyond my imagining. I placed my order and then had a disconcerting thought. We'd been asked to pay our board and room in cash, so when we landed in Kingston I'd changed all our money into Jamaican dollars. Several thousand American dollars made for a wad of Jamaican money about three inches thick, all of which was in my left front jeans pocket. Picture the sketchiest place in the sketchiest neighborhood you know. Now imagine a stranger walking in and pulling $50,000 in cash out of his pocket.

I was that guy.

"I'm going to die here," I thought. "I wonder if they'll find my body, or if I'll just disappear into the harbor?"

I paid with my smallest bill out of the three-inch wad, received my change and the cool drinks. Everyone in the store smiled and nodded to me as I left, and then turned back to their conversations.

If they saw the wet streak from the sweat running down my spine they were too polite to laugh.

At that point in my life, Kingston, Jamaica was the scariest place I'd ever been, with the possible exception of Franklin Avenue in St. Paul the fall of 1974, when I'd lost my spare change to a couple massive and massively drunken individuals. Of course, at that time I was eighteen, so I think I can be excused for not knowing the wrong time to be in the wrong place.

I didn't have that excuse this time. I thought the neighborhood was awful and looking back I can say that I was underestimating its pervasive menace. The church was in a compound with sturdy walls around it, and on one memorable day we huddled more or less in the middle as about fifty guys with knives and broken bottles conducted what may have been interpretive dance, but certainly looked like a melee. I was responsible for my wife, mother-in-law, my three children, and a half-dozen teenagers who didn't belong to me. In hindsight I can't believe how stupid I was.

The third day we were there, Sister Julia arranged for me to meet with a local Peace Corps representative. After we dropped off our team at work we drove across town to a small, pleasant house parked in the shade of some large trees. A compact grey haired lady came out to meet us and ushered us in. She was a school teacher from somewhere up North who'd joined the Peace Corps after retirement.

She was sweet and friendly, serving us juice and offering to have her cook prepare us breakfast. I'm sure she was a sincere person who desperately wanted to make things better in Kingston, but I couldn't help thinking that between her Peace Corps stipend and her retirement income she was living a considerably better life in Jamaica than she would have had in Bismarck or Detroit.

Sister Julia was disappointed in me because I didn't want to stay for breakfast; I wanted to get back to the kids. The Peace Corps lady was a little taken aback, too, but then she smiled and said, "I suppose, you never know what mischief a bunch of teenagers can get into if they're left alone."

She lost me there. No, I thought, I'm not scared of what sort of mischief the little scamps might get into, I'm worried that they might get killed or kidnapped.

I was relieved to get back to the church and to get back to work.

As the week dragged on, we started attracting more of an audience. Nobody actually helped, but local teenagers came and hung out with us. There was this one kid. Thirty years later I still think about him. I was rehanging a rotten wood door on an outdoor shower. This, among other things, involved killing a scorpion that tumbled out of its nest in the doorjamb. An old man who lived nearby was supervising my work when this teenage boy wandered over to provide his input. I don't remember what he said, but it made me laugh. I've never been scared by teenage boys and I was enjoying his company but the old man suddenly flew off the handle and launched into a tirade, speaking far to fast for me to understand.

The boy looked at him, smiled, and with charming arrogance said, "What you gonna do, old man, call the police? The police, they be scared of me."

Was it true? Might well have been—he had the sort of easy charisma that could have had him running the Kingston version of the Jets or the Sharks. Later that day he gave us a gymnastics exhibition doing flips and cartwheels across the broken-glass studded parking lot.

I wanted to bring him home with us, send him to a good school, and help him run for senator. That didn't happen. If he wasn't dead in a decade, by now he's a tired middle-aged man, most likely working a job that doesn't feed his body or his soul.

That's the sin, and I don't use that word lightly, of badly done economic development work. It's so wasteful. Wasteful of heart and soul, of body and blood, of potential and promise. Kids are kids, no matter where they're born.

When I think of the Mozarts, Einsteins, and Maria Curies who have died of malaria or endured a few decades of labor in banana plantations or coal mines because there was no road that green-lighted potential over picking the right parents, it makes me scream.

I've been screaming since 1986.

We finished our week of work. My charismatic juvenile delinquent came with a few other folks to see us off, and we headed back north, through Spanish Town and back on the main road to Montego Bay. Up to this point the kids had been in Jamaica a week and hadn't even dipped their toes in salt water. Since we were on the wrong side of the country from the airport and our flight left early in the day, I decided a night in a resort hotel would make sense.

When I called to set up reservations I explained who I was traveling with, in hopes of getting adjoining rooms so I could keep an eye on my own juveniles. The resort apparently shared the same concerns, because for a little less money than hotel rooms they put us up in a seaside villa with five bedrooms, a swimming pool, a cook, a maid, and a houseboy. The contrast between what we left and what we arrived at was cruel.

One of our sixteen year olds, a young woman I'd never thought of as particularly sensitive, sat at the dining room table and quietly sobbed when the maid wouldn't let her help clear the dinner dishes.

Of course, it wasn't all guilt and angst.

We were about a mile from the resort headquarters. As typical American teenagers our kids usually would have found that distance impossible to transit on foot, but for some reason they were eager to walk along the beach instead of getting a ride.

I found out the reason when my mother-in-law came back from a stroll and informed me that the resort's nude beach was right next to us.

She told my wife about a man reclining on a towel. "And he was brown all over," was what I heard as I came into the room.

An educational trip from beginning to end.

That was a long time ago. We went back to various parts of Jamaica three more times. I've been on the back roads of Haiti, Uganda, and some of the sketchier parts of many other countries. I've developed several theories for what sustainable economic development looks like. Keep in mind, I'm not talking about tidying up after a hurricane or earthquake, when you just need all hands on deck to get something done. Sometimes the right thing to do is send in the Marines, with helicopters and bulldozers. I'm talking about going to a place and changing lives for the better for generations to come.

First, if locals aren't doing half the work and providing half the plan, you're wasting your time. The other half of, "you don't care about people you don't know," is, "you don't care about what you haven't paid for." At Wesley church we wouldn't have been worried about graffiti on the walls of the church if there'd been a few grumpy adults in the neighborhood who'd spent their evenings helping to paint. In fact, if I'd been able to convince my budding drug lord/prime minister to pick up a paintbrush the whole neighborhood might really have been transformed.

> If locals aren't doing half the work and providing half the plan, you're wasting your time.

In addition, the stunning arrogance of do-gooders sailing into a place and telling the people what they need is usually wrong-headed and almost always counterproductive. Does it take longer to make a decision and implement a plan when there are more and more folks involved? Well, yeah, but we've been working on that whole, "love thy neighbor as thyself," thing for a couple of thousand years now, without getting all the bugs worked out, so it's probably okay to spend some time getting things right.

Second, the government is always part of the solution or part of the problem. That's just the way it is. Granted, a dozen Midwesterners with sunburned knobby knees aren't going to be able to do much about good governance in the developing world, but most of us do vote. When we're at home we should do what we can to keep our government from supporting the wrong folks and doing dumb stuff. For instance, if there's a South American country with a choice between a budding Commie and a thug in a uniform who's in the pocket of United Fruit, that may seem like a choice between the lesser of two evils. Well, here's an idea—why don't we let the people in that country decide, without any help from us, the CIA or our 82nd Airborne?

> The government is always part of the solution or part of the problem.

Yeah, I know, we've been meddling in other countries politics since before Teddy Roosevelt and, really, how has that worked out for us? Heck, we've managed to ruin a half dozen countries just because we have an inordinate fondness for cocaine and meth—imagine what we'd have done if marijuana sales had been part of profit picture for the tobacco companies.

Another reason not to meddle in other countries is that it makes us feel bad about ourselves for no real purpose. Truman didn't lose China to the Communists—Chiang Kai-shek was really bad at running a country and he worked himself out of a job. We didn't keep our military from winning in Vietnam—the South Vietnamese government was massively corrupt and incompetent and killed enough of their own people that those remaining turned to the Communists.

Afghanistan has no real tradition of good governance, and the last time Iraq had a solid government was in 1228. Winning every battle doesn't mean anything if there is no one competent available to run the country. Yes, horrible things happened in all those countries, and we intervened to make the horrible things stop. But quite often we've made things worse. That's because in a war, who has the clearest vision is sometimes more important than who has the biggest guns.

Remember, government is always part of the problem or part of the solution. Anyone who tells you something different probably thinks Yoko Ono is a musician, rather than a performance artist, and shouldn't be trusted with anything requiring insight.

Third, if you're not planning on working yourself out of a job, you're doing it wrong. Every medical team that flies to Haiti should show teenagers how to bandage a wound or wrap a sprained ankle, and then they should bring a prospective med student back to the States, with the understanding that they would pay for their education by working in their home country. If you're pouring cement you should hand a trowel to the kid who's standing watching.

You know what I see as success? If, when the big one hits and California falls into the ocean Haiti, Liberia, and Sierra Leone send aid teams to help cope with the disaster.

That's the world I want to live in, one where we are able to transcend our past and move toward a future that makes sense.

I've been a Methodist my whole life. I should really be a Lutheran, but my grandfather fell in love with a Methodist and thus fell away from the true faith. So I'm stuck with Methodism and I'm stuck with one of the tenets of the denomination, a quote that is often attributed to John Wesley. He perhaps never said it, but he said enough stuff like it to still make it valid. "Do all the good you can. By all the means you can. In all the ways you can. In all the places you can. At all the times you can. To all the people you can. As long as ever you can."

What he certainly didn't say was, "Do stuff that makes you look good but makes no lasting impact for the better."

Lesson 5
Quit Your Bad Ideas

I can't make scrambled eggs on a grill. I'm guessing that you don't really see that as a problem, but it's kind of a thing for me. I have fully resolved my remaining omelet issues and can make the difference easily discernible between eggs over-easy and eggs medium. I can even take an order for "eggs, lightly basted," without panicking. But scrambled eggs on a grill is just beyond me.

The first day I opened the café I only had two customers. It wasn't until about the third day that someone ordered scrambled eggs. I hadn't really practiced them, because, really, how hard can it be?

Pretty hard.

I mixed up some eggs and slapped them on the grill. They cooked in about nine seconds. They looked, and I'm sure tasted, much like a yellowish-green hockey puck. I kept practicing, but only about two people a week order scrambled eggs so I never had quite enough practice to master the art.

After a while I left hockey puck behind, but never really approached fluffy. I even watched YouTube videos on how to make scrambled eggs on a grill, which should indicate my level of desperation. After about a year and a half, meaning well over 100 orders of mediocre eggs, I finally stepped back and thought about my food booth fiasco.

Let me explain.

Years ago my wife and I were in charge of our church youth group, and we were trying to raise money by having a food booth at a local carnival. The way it worked was all the groups selling food showed up in the morning and whacked together a rudimentary booth of 2x4s and plywood. I thought there must be a better way, so I spent a day in my shop making a booth of steel tubing fastened together with slip pins. I assembled it and it wobbled back and forth like a drunken duckling. I added a few cross braces and tried again.

Still wobbled.

It took about a day and a half of construction efforts before I stood back and said, "What I have here is a bad idea. I can work as hard as I want, dress it up as much as possible, but it will still be a bad idea."

Ask yourself whether some abject quitting might be just the ticket.

I threw the iron on the scrap pile to use for other projects, and when the day of the carnival arrived I whacked together a booth out of 2x4s and plywood.

That experience was worth another year in college. I've gotten used to taking a step back and spending a few moments wondering if I'm in the depths of a bad idea and some abject quitting is just the ticket.

Now I just make the scrambled eggs in an omelet pan.
A little cream, a little butter, start them cooking at the same
time I start the bacon, and keep the temperature low and
the stirring incessant. I remove them shortly before I think
they're done and, bada bing, we're there.

I can still have a tough time, knowing when to quit, but
I've had several refresher courses.

Lesson 6
Know What You Don't Know

I'm going to blame Dan Hasslen for the next chapter in my life. That isn't really fair, but I've always felt that fairness is overrated.

One of the ways we raised money to take kids to Jamaica was by serving congregational dinners of pulled pork. We didn't know we were making pulled pork. That was thirty years ago, long before everyone in Minnesota was talking about stuff like pulled pork.

But I was a hog farmer at the time so the raw material was available, it was a product that a bunch of high school kids could turn out, and my wife had developed a recipe that people seemed to love. In particular, one good church-goer named Dan Hasslen raved about the stuff, and every time he came through the lunch line he'd say, "You should sell this stuff."

As time went on, more and more people requested pork for weddings and graduations. We kept donating it to the church, but selling it to other folks.

I was casting about for something to add a little profit and diversity to my farming enterprise, and the food business seemed like an easy segue.

That by itself was a mistake. Looking back at the various enterprises I've been involved with, the food industry is probably the most challenging and for us, it was a freakin' disaster. Perhaps one could call it a learning experience. I hope it was, because it was the equivalent of at least one Harvard education—in cost and educational benefits.

So here's what we did. If you're going to sell food to others, you need to produce that food in an approved commercial kitchen.

We didn't have one.

But our school had one, and they shut down at 3:00 p.m. every afternoon. We struck a deal to bring the kitchen fully up to code, spending a few thousand dollars and a significant amount of labor to do so, and in exchange we used the kitchen once a week or so from 4:00 p.m. until midnight.

That part of the plan was a pretty good idea, and if we would have stuck with that it could have been a nice little sideline, generating a few thousand dollars in profit and giving us something to do during slow times on the farm.

We worked incredibly hard. I can still remember coming home from the school kitchen at midnight, smelling of cooked pork and barbecue sauce, with my feet aching from long hours of standing, and my wrists throbbing from cutting meat and stirring. I'd drive by the bar on my way out of town and see a dozen cars and pickups there. That was the moment where I decided that if I ever did make any money in my life, I wouldn't apologize for it.

It turns out that hasn't really been a problem.

I'm a quarter of a century older now and looking back, I can point out any number of mistakes I made in the pulled pork world.

First, I wasn't a very good boss. I had a really clear idea of what I wanted done and how I wanted it done, but I didn't communicate it very well and I wasn't at all ruthless enough in enforcing my vision. I think this is the enterprise that taught me the most about how not to be a boss.

You know that great line the Kennedys used, "Some men see things as they are and ask 'why?' I dream things that never were and say, 'Why not?'" I remember hearing it, when Teddy Kennedy quoted it at Bobby Kennedy's funeral. I still get chills when I think of the moment. But the derivation of the quote is George Bernard Shaw, from his play "Back to Methuselah." The line is something the serpent whispers to Eve. That should give one pause. The line is one *the serpent whispers to Eve.* George Bernard Shaw was a smart guy, with a very cold eye. Dreamers are a vital part of any claim to progress, but a few folks with cold eyes and a grasp of reality are kind of important, too.

At this point in my life I lacked a cold eye.

The biggest evidence of that was the ways I put people in positions where they would not, could not, succeed.

> Dreamers are vital to progress, but so are folks with cold eyes and a grasp of reality.

We had two paid employees, along with a monumental amount of work done by my wife and me, and a certain amount of coerced labor from our children. One of the employees I'd known basically my whole life. He'd worked with us on the farm for years; when the world changed and there was no longer a place for a small breeding stock firm I looked for a way to keep him with us.

I'm not even sure I asked him if he wanted to stay, which was my first mistake. He was a great guy, honest, good at meeting people, and a very hard worker. But, he'd never borrowed money in his life, never made a budget, never purchased a house or made an expenditure larger than buying a vehicle.

It gets worse. I'm always comfortable with changing positions or even directions, while he was considerably more linear. He went on the road peddling our product and did a terrific job selling it. Our plan was to market our goods and build up a route and pick up business by selling products from other small outfits like ours. It was a pretty good idea, although perhaps one whose time had not yet come. I was busy running the farm that was supporting this entire enterprise. I let him set the prices, pick the products, negotiate with stores, decide on the route and do the store demonstrations.

He simply lacked the experience to set the prices at a point where we could break even. Or maybe he set the prices at a point where we were competitive, and those weren't high enough to let us turn a profit. I can't emphasize enough the need for a cold eye. I'm barely able to catalog all the dubious decisions and obstacles that were glossed over by hope and ambition. Our meat was healthy, with no additives, but it wasn't something that could be classified as "organic," which meant we were excluded from a number of potential outlets.

We'd started out marketing our own meat in an effort to diversify, but ended up having our product made in a factory in St. Paul because government regulations were just too onerous. We were sandbagged by our only competitor, whose owner was also the owner of a large chain of grocery stores where our product was supposed to be stocked. The order was canceled at the last second and we ended up having to give, literally, a ton of meat to food kitchens in order that it not go to waste.

My biggest surprise was that the coup de grâce was administered by our very own government.

What many people don't know is that every time there is a change in a product, the label has to reflect that. We started using a leaner cut of meat, which affected the nutrition data on the label. We sent the label to Washington for approval, something we'd done a half dozen times before. This process involved somebody whose very existence still makes me crazy. His, or her, job title is "facilitator" and what they do is put your application on the desk of the person who approves it, and makes sure it doesn't get lost. So, we were paying a private company to make sure a government employee did what they were getting paid to do.

I gritted my teeth a little just writing that sentence.

We did the label updates a half-dozen times for minor changes. This last one though, came back rejected. Why? Because, the functionary in charge had decided that our product name, "Olson's Pleasant Valley Farms Country Style Barbecued Pork," was deceptive, because the product wasn't made in the country.

I wrote the Department of Agriculture a letter saying that the product couldn't be made in the country, because it needed to be made in a federally inspected facility. The letter was a little more elaborate than that, because without an approved label we were out of business and we were hemorrhaging money even when we were selling product. Frantic would be an understatement. The manager of the plant that was producing our product thought that this was the work of our giant competitor, but I prefer to see it as simple incompetence. I made a huge fuss—the "Star Tribune" business editor wrote an article about it, Senator Paul Wellstone assigned a staff member to it and a year later, his office received a letter of apology from the Department of Agriculture.

In the end, everything turned out okay. I'd been so worried about our employees but they went on to jobs they liked better, with larger paychecks. I worked harder and paid off all the accumulated bills, although it took about a decade to get the last loan behind us.

> You need to know what you don't know, and sometimes you need to know when it's time to quit.

An economic development agency had given us quite a bit of advice and some money. In exchange for them writing off the money portion, I wrote an utterly candid report on everything that had gone wrong. It was painful to write, but I've always thought that failed experiments should get just as much publicity as the ones that succeed, because they can show the path not to follow. I ran into the director a few years later and he told me that they still used my report as an in-house cautionary tale.

What did I learn? Well, the boss always needs to know what's going on. You can't be afraid to ask questions that make people uncomfortable. You need to poke your nose in places and, more importantly, you need to be willing to answer questions that make you uncomfortable. You need to know what you don't know, and sometimes you need to know when it's time to quit. And you need to know, to the depths of your soul, that no one cares about your business as much as you do. Talk is cheap and so is advice.

I remember when that last one sunk in. I'd spent the day doing product demonstrations at a big event set up by a state economic development agency. I'd given away about 50 pounds of pork in bite sized portions without really generating any sales, mainly because most of the samples went to retired people with nothing better to do than wander the aisles, other desperate businesspeople, and any number of local, state, and federal employees who smiled encouragingly and gave vast compliments.

At the end of the day there was a reception for all the exhibitors and the representatives of various agencies. I walked into the reception tired and a little discouraged. I looked around and everyone else was into their second drink. There was much laughter and camaraderie. That's when it dawned on me.

These were good people and they all did want me to succeed, but it was like the old story of the difference between a hen and a hog for breakfast. The hen contributes, but the hog is committed. I was the only one in the room who was truly committed, and it changed forever the way I look at the people who do development work.

I drank half a beer and headed for home. Sunk in despair for my failing business I made a left turn on a green light, thinking it was a green arrow, and was blindsided by a pickup charging towards me in the other lane. Sitting on the curb being checked out by the EMTs while staring at my wife's wrecked car did distract me from my problems.

At least for a while.

Lesson 7
Avoid Stomachaches

About five years after the barbecued pork debacle, I received a phone call from a guy I'd never met. He'd gotten my name from someone I did know and was wondering if I would be interested in being part of a group of guys who wanted to start up an ethanol plant.

At that time a product called MTBE (methyl tertiary butyl ether) was being used to enhance the octane rating of gasoline. It worked well for that, except it was a carcinogen, water soluble, and persistent in the environment.

These are all bad things, so the idea was to replace MTBE with ethanol, which is just alcohol.

For perhaps the first time in my life, where I lived was the ideal location for an economic development project, all because we were a long way from Chicago.

Let me explain.

Historically, the amount of actual money that I could sell my crops for was based on what those crops would sell for in Chicago, less the cost of transportation.

That system began 150 years ago. The Illinois and Michigan Canal opened in 1848, which helped ship large quantities of grain cheaply to the population centers of the East and coincidentally, there were large quantities of grain being produced in the region all around Chicago.

For no better reason than that, the price of grain all over America became based on what that same product would sell for in Chicago

So, if you wanted to make ethanol out of corn, the advantage went to the place with the cheapest corn that was closest to where the product was used. You can't grow corn everywhere—there's a reason the Midwest is called the Corn Belt. My home had the dubious honor of the cheapest corn in America.

These days, when we're filling the Gulf of Mexico with dirt and it seems like the entire Midwest is planted to corn, it's easy to forget that ethanol used to be seen by pretty much everyone as something that was good for the environment.

I didn't know much about ethanol or anything about investing, but the project seemed to tick the box marked, "What the hell, let's try it," so I went to the next meeting.

The meeting was held in the town fire-hall in Milbank, SD, just across the border from Big Stone County. I didn't know any of the men in the room except that they were all the sort of men I'd known my whole life. Farmers, every one of them, largely successful, with tanned forearms, pale foreheads and an air of competence. They were all from South Dakota and it had been suggested that a little regional diversity would be in order so they were looking for a couple of guys from Minnesota to join their group. My name had come up.

I don't remember what topics came up at that first meeting, because over the next year there were a lot of meetings. This was pretty exciting stuff—it was the beginnings of the ethanol plant boom and we were in the forefront. The person advising us, Steve Sershen, was a type I'd never spent much time around.

When I was growing up, almost all my family members were nurses, farmers, or teachers. There were no bums in the group, but no high-powered business executives either. Everyone worked hard for their money, but that wasn't very much money.

Steve had a career in banking, among other things, and had retired early, moved back to South Dakota, and eked out a six digit income helping farmers get various enterprises up and running. He brought expertise and a bit of an edge to the meetings. A quote he often used when trying to discourage flights of fancy was, "The leading edge is often the bleeding edge." It's often not the first person who tries something who makes money, it's the third or fourth person, after the expensive bugs have been worked out.

I was in my late forties at this time and it was the first time in my life that I realized how much purposeful complexity went into running a major business. I know that makes me sound stupid, but, hey, the truth hurts. I can castrate a hog in thirty seconds, I can write a novel, I can shingle a house and I can get people to pay me $1,000 just for talking for twenty minutes, but I freely admit there are a number of things I'm fascinated to watch but cannot do.

Brain surgery, waltzing, and following through on the three hundred steps of beginning a large scale business from scratch are a few that come immediately to mind.

I wasn't the only one in the room mystified. Everyone else was successful on some level or another, but we were talking about $50 million in investments, and about that much in a year to run it. So we were talking about serious money, and plenty of room to screw things up.

I understand why business schools teach about ultimate priorities ... things like, "the only thing that matters is profit," or "the only thing that matters is the shareholders' return on investment." It's bad for society at large, but logical for the business. In the world most of us live in, stress often comes from the continual struggles between priorities. You have a job deadline but it's your kid's third grade Christmas program, you want to live in a shack while you write the great American novel but your kids want to go to college, a potentially valuable business partner is an absolute asshole ... the opportunities for complexity and hard choices are nearly infinite. Picking one overriding priority takes away a lot of the pain.

Our proposed ethanol plant would provide a place to sell your corn, but it would also provide valuable tax base and some solid blue-collar jobs. The guys on the board represented two different states and several different counties, and we all wanted it located where it could do our own people the most good. Of course, putting it in the wrong place might doom the whole project and no amount of good wishes would change that. We developed a mantra, repeated at virtually every meeting. Someone would say, "We'll go where the facts take us," and everyone would nod grimly and privately surrender the idea of selling a worthless back forty for the plant site.

I really enjoyed these meetings. I didn't have a lot in common with most of the people in the room, but I'm used to that. I lead an odd life, with an unusual set of priorities, and that's just the way things are. The group wasn't exactly like a platoon from a WWII movie, with a cowboy, a loud-mouth from Brooklyn and a doomed farm boy from Iowa. We were all farmers from Minnesota and South Dakota, but even that level of homogeneity allowed for a significant range of political affiliations and income disparities. I confess I didn't get to know many of them well—some of the guys would go out for beers after meetings, but I was never really invited, because I'm a guy who doesn't get invited for beers after work. I've never been completely sure why that is, but it's been a forty-year trend.

My guess is I was the poorest guy in the room. This was due in part to a recent catastrophic hailstorm, a hog-house fire, the fact that I was putting three kids through college, and because in a personality profile I scored in the bottom one percent of Americans in the category, "Motivated by money." Whatever the reason, I'd often come into a discussion with a slightly different point of view from some of the others. I think I did serve a purpose—let's face it, thirteen people just like me on the board and the project probably would have failed. A board without anyone like me wouldn't have been a good idea, either.

The main lesson I learned from this project is one that I first learned when I was fifteen and working off the farm for the first time in my life. At that time and place, if a young man wanted some money for gasoline and the pursuit of sin, the most common way to obtain it was by baling hay.

For you urban types, here's a short primer on animal agriculture. A modern dairy cow eats a ration a little bit more finely tuned than an Olympic athlete's. When I was a kid, part of that diet was alfalfa, put up in rectangular bales weighing, depending on the moisture content and mercy of the dairy farmer, between 50 and 100 pounds. Baling hay, turning the hay from a swathe in the field to a neatly stacked pile in the attic of a barn, was a labor-intensive business, usually requiring a half dozen people to move things along efficiently. The standard pay was either a penny a bale or a dollar an hour.

Here's where the lesson kicked in. If you were working for a good farmer, you wanted a penny a bale, while a poor farmer—the guy with wet hay, a rusty baler, and flat-tired hayracks, should be made to pay you a dollar an hour while you sit in the shade of a tractor tire watching him swear at his broken machinery. But the larger lesson is this. Work with competent people. Anything else is a waste of time. They may be friendly, saints, aloof, or complete pains in the ass, but if you can get competent, you can usually deal with the other stuff.

Life, business, economic development, all of it, really is just that simple. Competence wins, incompetence makes your stomach hurt.

The ethanol plant was a huge success. We'd hoped to provide thirty good jobs, raise the local price of corn by a dime a bushel, and maybe even make a little money. What actually happened is that I got my investment back in cash dividends the first year. The stock went up, split, and split again. Now, ten years later I've had about a 1,500% return on my investment. My $10,000 investment is now worth $60,000 and the plant is still employing people and still making money.

> Competence wins, incompetence makes your stomach hurt.

Which is kind of a pity.

Since the initial plants were such huge successes, it wasn't long before everyone wanted to build one. Most plants of the initial wave were built within a hundred miles of the border between Minnesota and South Dakota. This is where the cheapest corn in America is grown, there's access to natural gas pipelines, and it is close to the market for the dried distiller's grain, the main byproduct. The next wave of plants were built in places with fewer natural advantages. Because there was so much ethanol hitting the market, the goal of simply reducing the use of MTBE was replaced with the idea of powering America through ethanol.

As a result we've slapped biodiversity in the face and filled big chunks of our lakes, rivers, and the Gulf of Mexico with toxic sludge. The Law of Unintended Consequences has struck once again.

As a rule, booms are stupid. I know, if you get in the game at the right time, a boom is the best place to make a lot of money fast, but booms are perhaps the biggest initiators of unintended consequences, and the mess they make of society can take a long time to straighten out. I remember when ethanol was going big and plants were starting up all over. I was talking to a banker about this and that, and he mentioned that he'd gone to a stock sale for a new plant and he'd had to fight his way to the front of the line to put his money down. I winced internally, but it was his money, not mine. Plus, he was a banker, he should know all about risks. I thought long and hard about saying something, but in the end I chose to say nothing. That path has seldom gotten me in trouble.

That plant went belly-up and the investors lost all their money. If I remember correctly, the people who bought it out for pennies on the dollar went belly-up as well.

What's interesting is that people often talk about the damage a bust does, but there isn't as much attention paid to the damage that happens during a boom.

As I write this, we're seeing that played out in the oil fields in North Dakota where the existing infrastructure,

> As a rule, booms are stupid.

both physical and societal, was hammered to its knees by the vast influx of people and money during the oil rush. Now that the boom is tapering off, the longtime residents of the region have to deal with the wreckage left behind.

And there was no need for it. I'm a firm believer in capitalism (well, a semi-firm believer), I like to see people making money, and I really enjoy seeing people making money in a place that has been ignored for years. Still, the North Dakota oil boom is a cautionary tale.

I'm kind of an agnostic on the whole fracking thing. I'm willing to believe there is a solid chance of substantial environmental damage from fracking, and I'm willing to be convinced that the damage could be mitigated and lessened by sensible precautions. So this is the place where a reasonable government would stand up on its hind legs and say, "Let's all take a deep breath. The oil has been there for millions of years and it'll wait while we sort things out."

Of course, that sort of thing doesn't happen all that often, because elected officials need to be, you know, elected. Standing in the way of progress and profits can end up with the average representative buried under a tidal wave of money. So, instead of making a principled stand for science, reason, and moderation—positions that are never particularly popular in American life, the elected officials in North Dakota could have just said, "No oil wells unless you also capture all the natural gas."

It would have been an easy argument to frame—wells in North Dakota flared off a billion dollars a year in natural gas during the height of the boom and while it is possible to capture almost all of that, it takes a while to set up the infrastructure. Throwing away that amount of money would be a compelling argument even to a guy who goes back for seconds at the spotted owl buffet. The oil companies following the boom wouldn't have liked it, but on the other hand, if you're near someone who's leaping up and down yelling, "Buy now," like a used car salesman in a plaid coat, you probably should keep your hand on your wallet.

Why wasn't this done? I dunno. I think it would have worked. Over the years I've gained some confidence in my skill at framing things so everyone can feel like a winner. God help me, this is what I do. I wish it wasn't—I wish I could sing, dance, and write sonnets, but that isn't the hand I was dealt. Instead, if you put me in a room with a big table and people with serious disagreements I make things better. Unless things go south.

In which case if I'm involved, things can go very, very south indeed. As my wife occasionally says, "Please don't tell that story, because I hate for people to know what you're capable of."

So I won't tell that story here.

Lesson 8
Know When to Dig a Deeper Trench

The ethanol plant was a big success. In an effort to build on that, a few guys, including me, starting toying with the idea of getting some wind turbines in our county. Big Stone County, as I've explained four or five hundred times to any number of people, is the last, best, undeveloped wind resource in Minnesota.

A few miles west of us in South Dakota is a range of hills called the Coteau Des Prairies. South of us, when the hills take a left and wander into Minnesota, they're called the Buffalo Ridge. And, the entire length is dotted with wind turbines, being in kind of a sweet spot, where there is maximum sustained wind close to power lines that lead to areas of massive energy usage. Big Stone County isn't quite that good, but it's pretty good.

Now, some people hate wind turbines. A lot of that hate comes from geography, history, and taste. One of the first sites of a massive wind turbine farm was in Altamont Pass in California. It was made up of wind turbines that spun as fast as a window fan and it was located on a major bird migration route. Much of the data you see on bird kills from wind turbines is based on data gathered at that site, with those wind turbines.

Some people think they're ugly. I kind of like the way they look. They're impressive in an industrial-dinosaurs-walking-the-earth kind of way. A massive presence looming over the horizon, a little like a Hoover Dam on the prairie.

Not everyone agrees.

The sight of wind turbines was not particularly contentious in my area—this area is already used to industrial agriculture modifying the scenery, and the jobs and economic impact of wind farms were eagerly anticipated. I thought since we'd just come out the other side of a $50 million ethanol plant project, a few million for a wind farm in a place where no one would object to it would be easy.

I was completely wrong.

We ended up failing, more or less completely. It was a lesson to me in the same way the barbecued pork biz was a lesson, just a completely different lesson. It was my introduction to the world of politics and policy, along with a graduate school class in people doing things contrary to their best interests.

So here's the deal. Wind turbines are not a build-it-and-they-will-come kind of thing. Someone has to be willing to buy the electricity you produce, at a price that makes profit possible, and for that you need a power purchase agreement (PPA) from a utility.

Utilities are usually risk-averse. That's not a bad thing; you want the people who keep the lights on to err on the conservative side. On the other hand, I'm sure that dinosaurs were risk averse, too, and look what that got them. Evolve or die, baby, and hope the big meteor isn't coming your way.

There are a number of easy ways to make electricity— build a dam on a raging river, for example, or dig a hole in the ground and feed coal right into a boiler—the problem is that many of those easy methods aren't particularly good for the environment, not to mention children with asthma and salmon trying to procreate.

The sad truth is that "comfortable" is most people's default attitude and preference. If there are going to be substantive changes, quite often there either needs to be a seismic cultural change or a compulsion of some sort. Compulsion can be tricky.

The Law of Unintended Consequences is right up there with gravity and conservation of energy.

This leads me to the Big Stone Power plant. They started building the power plant when I was in high school, four decades ago. It's across the state line from where I live. My entire adult life, when the weather conditions are right, I've been able to see an orange-yellow streak in the sky coming from that power plant. I didn't see it everyday, but I saw it pretty often. Coal combustion is an easy way to make electricity, but there are significant downsides to that.

When I was on the first board of directors of the ethanol plant start-up we had a briefing from representatives of the Big Stone Power plant, because we were going to get some of their excess steam, and they told us they were going to expand the plant AND install up to date pollution control equipment.

I was pretty excited by the prospect because of that orange-yellow streak.

But then I had my idea. It might not have been just mine; this all happened a decade or more ago. The plan was that we, our little group, knew that permitting a coal-fired power plant expansion was going to be tricky, even if the expanded plant was going to cut sulfur and mercury emissions by 90%.

If the plant had been willing to sequester carbon dioxide and perhaps commit ritual suicide it still would have been tricky.

The utilities knew it was going to be tricky. If my memory is correct, and it may not be, they told us they had set aside $10 million for the permitting process. That's the figure I recall, but even if my memory is incorrect, they planned on spending a lot of money to get this done.

Our plan was that if the utilities would agree to buy wind power from us they would be able to see that it would help their image. I thought they should build a wind farm in every county their transmission lines passed through. Shoot, I thought they should use some of the billions of British Thermal Units (Btu) they threw away every day to heat massive greenhouses, so the protestors would need to walk through a tunnel lined with green peppers and exotic endangered plants in order to get to the front desk.

Would it have been a better plan to not have any coal- fired power plants? Well, if you're thinking about the environment, you bet. If you're thinking about jobs, reliability, fitting into the existing infrastructure, least societal disruption, and least entrenched resistance, maybe it's less of a sure thing. The bottom line is, this was a decade or more ago and it's only been within the past year or so the renewables have made a quantum leap in cost effectiveness. No coal just wasn't an option that was presented.

I confess to some ulterior motives—I thought if we did get some wind farms up and running, and a distributed power infrastructure starting up, you could see that solar cell power was going to start coming on strong. All this meant that we would have within our reach a distributed power system using all renewables. The coal-fired plants would just die of their own dead weight and then no one would have to worry about spending their adult lives watching an orange-yellow streak in the sky.

So, maybe the utilities weren't stupid after all, maybe they feared the camel's nose under the tent, maybe they knew in their heart of hearts that they were dinosaurs with a meteor in the sky and that's why they didn't want to work with us.

Actually, they never even returned my phone calls. The public relations guy assigned to work in the county didn't return my phone calls.

Now that's bad. Although, I can name something that felt worse.

Two separate events took place about this time. I was elected to be a county commissioner. That's a group of five people in a county who are responsible for the quality of the roads, the size of the Family Services budget, and a few dozen other things. The pay isn't much—a thousand bucks a month plus money for health insurance, but there are a number of opportunities to give small nudges that can help move things in a useful direction.

There are also nearly infinite opportunities to feel the end of your life approaching as you sit in useless meetings, but that's another story. I ran for commissioner because of a conversation I had with someone who was going to run in my district. I asked her what she wanted most to accomplish if she was elected and she didn't have an answer. Really. Nothing popped into her head at all.

The non-answer rankled deep in my bones. Why in the hell would anyone run for public office unless they had a compelling cause they wanted to advance? I put off the decision as long as I could, but I eventually filed, campaigned, and won.

The county had set aside some economic development funds to help the wind turbine project, which meant I had to recuse myself from pretty much everything involving alternative energy. I declared my conflict of interest to the board, and to the county attorney and followed his guidance to keep myself out of trouble.

The second event was that I had lunch with an acquaintance. Our kids had been in school at the same time and we vaguely knew each other the way you do in a small town. She'd left the area years before but had returned recently as an employee of an environmental group.

I'd always thought of myself as an environmentalist, although as it turned out, environmentalists did not agree with that self-assessment. I did know that I was the closest thing you're going to find to a lefty in rural Minnesota elected office. I was the most liberal county commissioner in my memory and about as liberal as you could be and still be elected.

During our lunch my acquaintance shared her implacable opposition to the power plant project and I shared that I was willing to let it advance if it meant renewable energy across Minnesota and an end to the orange-yellow streak in the skies above Big Stone County. I was troubled by the failure to do anything about capturing or converting the carbon dioxide from the larger power plant, but I thought the trade-off would be worth it, with other battles on the horizon to move closer to the ideal. I also mentioned that I had to step carefully because of the conflict of interest issue.

The next day I received a phone call from our county auditor. My acquaintance had stopped in and suggested I be impeached. If, from an excess of worry about appearances, I hadn't already spoken to the board and the county attorney I would have been in a great deal of trouble. Not that an end to my political career would have been any great agony, but the threat to my reputation, the thought of my friends and neighbors believing I'd been using taxpayer funds to enrich myself, was sickening.

I don't believe I'm overstating that it would have ruined my life, and destroyed the carefully cultivated image I have of myself. I have two issues with her actions. First, to do this dire thing so casually, to try to set in motion something so personally destructive, offended me greatly.

Second, it was stupid. Who did she think was going to replace me? Sure, she and I weren't perfect allies, but there were so many areas where we could have worked together, where our desired ends were perfectly aligned. Instead, she wanted me hounded from office. If she had succeeded, my replacement would have been someone worse.

I found it baffling ten years ago. I'm still baffled.

Despite the attempted character assassination, these were heady times in the wind industry. Wind turbines were springing up hither and yon, and it seemed possible to make money, provide jobs, and protect the environment all at the same time. It seemed like the beginning of the best of all possible worlds.

A quote I often think of is from the business advisor Tom Peters. He says, "Life is pretty simple: You do some stuff. Most fails. Some works. You do more of what works. If it works big, others quickly copy it. Then you do something else." This had worked in the ethanol biz, but our efforts fell flat with wind energy.

There were two interesting reasons for that. First, we were in the position of dealing with a monopoly. We needed to sell the power to the organization that controlled the power line in our territory, and they weren't interested at all. They wanted a huge, coal-fired power plant, and they didn't want to fool around with anything else. So, with our right flank firmly on fire, we also found ourselves attacked on our left flank, stymied by some environmental groups who also didn't want the utilities to work with us. They didn't want even a sliver of a silver lining from any power plant upgrades. If the price of a series of clean energy generating enterprises was the expansion of a coal-fired plant, no matter what pollution control upgrades were made, they weren't interested. Strange bedfellows indeed.

I understand the position of the people who squashed our plans, I really do. I understood it at the time, too. But it was a harsh pill to swallow, with the orange-yellow streak still crossing the sky above my head, and with no new jobs, no distributed energy system, and a sadly deliberate crushing of the optimistic, entrepreneurial spirit that had been burgeoning in our area. What's harder is that the crushing happened partially at the hands of good people who would ordinarily have wanted us to succeed.

The pain isn't mine alone.

Another thing about those folks who made my life miserable for a few months—those are people I don't call. That's a bigger deal than you might think.

> Clever insults are fun, but they're a minefield for productive long-term results.

If you lead a complicated life, with a lot of that life in the public sphere, there is always a need to build coalitions, to gather insights, and to build a bigger tent to draw more folks in. Some folks I chose not to bring into my tents, and that's a pity.

I'm not proud of that. I try to not dwell on the past, but when I have flashbacks to being called a whore and having letters to the editor advance the notion that I was on the payroll of big business, I tend to freeze up. I don't bad-mouth anyone, at least not by name, I don't hinder their projects, I try not to harm them in any way. There are just a few people and groups who are no longer in my Rolodex. Although they probably don't care, they've lost a voice in any number of things I'm involved with, which is a significant downside.

I rewrote this section about five times, and deleted it in its entirety a couple of times, but in the end I decided that just because the truth isn't flattering doesn't mean it isn't the truth. If you're going to have a dispute with someone about a particular issue, rude is effective only when you're confident you're never going to have to work with that person again. It can be fun to think of clever insults, but it's also a minefield for productive long-term results.

> When you're being attacked from two different directions, dig a deeper trench.

There isn't really a happy ending to this story, but it's not all dark. As I write this, eleven years later, the orange-yellow streak appears to be gone. With the election of President Obama, long stagnated environmental standards have been tweaked and the Big Stone Power plant just completed an expensive retrofit to clean up what comes out of the stack. That's a good thing, but there's still nothing done with the carbon dioxide and the other downsides of coal, there are still no upgrades to the grid, and there are still no giant turbines generating power and hope spinning in the skies where I live.

The lesson I took from this experience is simply this. When you're being attacked from two different directions, you need a deeper trench.

There is another lesson I took from this, and the illustration of it came from an unexpected source.

My wife is the director of a center for adults with intellectual disabilities. What that means is the folks who fifty years ago were warehoused in state institutions, and one hundred years ago were living in the attics of their parents' homes, now come to work every morning, doing things like shredding old documents, cleaning houses, and building furniture. Robin's job is difficult, valuable work. I'm always in awe of the people who can do that for years and retain their passion for doing it better.

A couple of decades ago Robin and I went together to Minneapolis—I don't remember the reason I went along. It was some nifty cultural event like a football game or a touring Broadway play I imagine, but before we could get to the fun stuff my wife had to attend a three hour seminar that was scheduled for the same day. I tagged along because we'd already checked out of the hotel room and I didn't have anything better to do.

The speaker was a piece of work. If I remember correctly, he had a huge feathered earring, a crew cut, and some other odd fashion choices. He was there to speak on how to work with people with disabilities. One of his qualifications was that he had a son with Down Syndrome. I didn't pay attention to much of what he said, but my ears did perk up at this phrase. "Pick the hill you're willing to die for," he said, "Take what you can get, closest to what you want."

> An unrelenting need to get everything you ask for often has the opposite effect.

There's nothing new about that—I've heard the same thing in different forms at many different times. Why his particular version stuck in my head is difficult to understand. I suppose simply because it seemed so practical.

This is a lesson so many smart people don't seem to internalize, and they should, because an unrelenting need to get everything you ask for quite often has the opposite effect. Sure, every now and then a Lenin or a

Hitler manages to bend the world to their wishes, but not very often.

If you were a Goldwater Republican in the Sixties, you have some responsibility for Lyndon Johnson's Great Society; if you were part of the riots in Chicago in 1968, Richard Nixon and Watergate are partly your fault; if you were a protest voter for Ralph Nader in Florida, you and Paul Wolfowitz are to blame for the invasion of Iraq; and as a Tea Party stalwart, any excesses of Obamacare can be laid directly at your feet.

> Ideas come from the edges, but progress comes from the middle.

Ideas come from the edges, but progress comes from the middle.

Take what you can get, closest to what you want, and get up the next day and continue the fight. Everyone does need to pick the hill they're willing to die for, because everyone has different triggers and priorities. If you're willing to die for every hill, that's fine, it's your choice. But you're going to die alone.

Lesson 9
Talk to the Enemy

A few years ago, an organization asked me it I wanted to put on my suit, go to Washington DC, in July, and do it for free. Sounded like crazy talk to me, but what is even crazier is that I talked myself into it.

Here's the deal. I was contacted and asked if I wished to be part of a lobbying effort to get the Clean Air Act renewed. My first thought was, that's crazy. Why would anyone need to lobby to get the Clean Air Act renewed? Then I stumbled upon a YouTube video of Representative Joe Barton of Texas saying he hadn't seen any evidence that mercury was bad for you.

I sighed deeply and booked my ticket.

I'd never done anything like this before and I didn't really know what to expect, or in fact why I had been contacted, but I was willing to saddle up and take my best shot. The organization I was working with had planned

for enough people from the Upper Midwest to call on all
our elected representatives, the theory being that we'd get
a better reception if we were actual constituents. The folks
from Minnesota were very fired up to visit with Senators
Franken and Klobuchar. I thought it seemed like a dumb
idea, but I wasn't management, I was labor, so I was willing
to go along.

It's not that I'm not fond of Klobuchar and Franken. I
think Minnesota is lucky to have those two for senators, I
just thought that the chances of either of them voting not
to renew the Clean Air Act were fairly slim. Why should
we waste our time, and theirs, giving them our spiel for
saving the environment?

That was a minor annoyance, but what really wound
me up was that no one wanted to go to talk to John Kline.

Representative John Kline is a reasonably conservative Republican. Not so very long ago he would have been
considered very conservative, but the bar for that has been
raised so high Genghis Khan would have some trouble getting over it.

Still, I was there on the behalf of a lefty organization
and he's a conservative guy. The person who was from his
district was a young woman—either just out of high school
or in her first year or two of college, and it was looking
like she would be going to this guy's office on her own. She
was visibly nervous. I've been a dad for a long time, with
a couple of daughters who would have hated what she was
being asked to do, so I volunteered to go with her.

It was an hour before our appointment and I'd just
received a phone call from my wife. She was upset because
she'd received a phone call from a friend who had been
asked to check if I was, for lack of a better term, ideologi-
cally pure enough to be representing an environmental
organization.

It was a little late for that. I was halfway through my assigned meetings, so there was no longer time for a purge. I was cranky, what with it being Washington in July, and I was wearing a suit, and the phone call didn't help at all.

I was already feeling some tension with being labor and not management, because I was watching some members of our group show up late for meetings or blow them off completely—not a good way to influence people, let alone make friends. I understand that some people have a stronger sense of time than others, and I know about being culturally sensitive, but when the train's leaving, you need to be on board.

I retreated to a corner of the meeting room so I wouldn't sully the rest of the group with my impure presence, opened my laptop, and did some research.

Here's what I found. Representative Kline was on the committee that funded DARPA, the military research group that is generally credited with inventing the Internet, and a few other things. A current priority of the military was finding a way to make our forces more energy independent, because in both Iraq and Afghanistan a significant number of casualties occurred just from transporting fuel through dicey terrain. Among other things, the military was looking at better batteries.

This is why that mattered. Energy storage is the silver bullet for alternative energies. There are lots of ways to make electricity, but only a few good ways to store it. Invent a good enough battery and hook it up to solar or wind farms, and you can chuck global warming down the chute and improve the lives of billions of people all over the world. Forget building transmission lines and giant power plants—a distributed energy system finally works.

John Kline might or might not care about global warming, but he had a proven record of caring about the troops, plus he had the ability to shunt a significant amount of money into funding research for a battery that could save our troops and save the planet. He was probably the most important person to talk to in Washington—and no one from our group wanted to.

In the end, I don't suppose it matters all that much. I'm sure I'm not the first person to make the connection between better batteries for our troops and better commercial energy storage. The young woman and I went to the meeting. Rep. Kline's office sent a guy to meet with us— I'm guessing someone who drew the short straw, because meeting with two low-level representatives from a not-very-important lefty organization probably wasn't the top priority for them either. Still, in a world where little things matter, choosing to do something poorly due to laziness or ideology is just a totally flawed concept.

After the meeting with the Kline representative, the young woman and I slogged back through humidity to headquarters. Later that afternoon, we were all supposed to attend a reception where someone who'd seen the President that week was supposed to be in attendance. I skipped out, caught the subway to the airport, and pounded down a beer next to my gate before I boarded the plane for home, limp from the heat and disappointment.

In a spasm of revenge that makes sense only to me, I refused to submit any bills for reimbursement to the organization that had doubted my purity and commitment.

That'll show 'em.

Lesson 10
Give Up If You Have To

Have you ever noticed that in movies six-fingered men are always the bad guys? In the Princess Bride the evil, six-fingered count stabs Inigo Montoya's father. And, of course, Hannibal Lector has six fingers and he eats people, which is way worse.

Garnett Kanne has six fingers, but he's a heck of a nice guy. Of course, the bad guys have their six fingers on one hand—Garnett has six, total. In 1978 he was harvesting corn and walked behind the corn picker and tripped on a corn stalk. He put his right hand out to catch himself. Unfortunately, where his hand landed was on a cast iron pulley spinning at 700 rpm. In less than a second his fingers were nipped off slick and clean and he was kneeling in the dirt clutching the bleeding stump. He tied a tourniquet with a shoestring and caught a ride to the hospital.

The next day a doctor stopped in the room and asked him if he was right handed. When Garnett said, "Yes," the doctor said, "Well, you're left-handed now." That was the end of his rehab and loss counseling. After a couple of surgeries to clean up bone fragments and tidy up the mess, they sent Garnett home and he went back to work.

Garnett lived in his brother's house for years, until age and encroaching infirmities sent him to a nursing home. His own house needed a roof, windows, and a paint job and he never quite got around to getting that all done. He's had a variety of jobs in his life, but for the past couple decades he's run a truck farm, raising vegetables and flowers that he sells at Farmer's Markets. He sang in the church choir and showed up to help shingle or wash windows as needed. For years he was the church lay leader, which meant he helped with communion, even when the shortage of four fingers caused his hold on the bread and wine to be a little tenuous. Once we had a pastor who liked to use a whole loaf of bread and just let people tear chunks off of it, which meant Garnett had to sort of stick his thumb in one end of the loaf and hold it up like a starchy lollypop.

My mom had been to the United Methodist Annual Conference where she had seen a plan for school desks that could be made and assembled in someone's shop, then shipped to places like Sierra Leone and Haiti—places where there appeared to be a shortage of schools, and school desks. For someone who had an irresistible urge to meddle, and a profound belief that education is a holy calling, her response was predictable. She handed the brochure to my father and turned him loose. He made his basement into a mini factory, and with help from the men's group at church, started shipping school desks around the world.

Garnett helped put the desks together for Operation Classroom, but there was something about the design that bothered him. These desks weren't going into a suburban living room. Garnett had never traveled to Haiti or Liberia, but he's a smart guy, and so he pointed out a weak spot in the design. It called for pine 1x4s for the legs, and pine just isn't very sturdy; it rots in wet weather and breaks under strain. But Garnett had some ash trees on his farm that he was getting sawed into lumber, and ash would make a fine leg for a desk. Ash is a little bit more than twice as strong as pine so it was just the ticket for a desk that might be placed on a dirt floor or subject to a lot more stress than it really should be.

One day Garnett pulled into my yard driving a thousand dollar pickup with two thousand dollars worth of hardwood in the back that he was planning on donating to the project.

It's always tough to tell with old farmers. Maybe he has a stack of cash that would choke a hippo, or a safety deposit box full of stocks and bonds, but to me he always seemed like he lived on what he could make, and the way he made it looked like a lot of work to me. The fact that he was willing to contribute so much, when he didn't really have all that much himself seemed like a great story to tell.

And telling stories is what I do.

We dreamed up the idea of following a desk from being a tree in Garnett's wood lot to having little kids start doing their homework on it in Haiti. It took a while to pull off—I was going to go on a trip to Liberia with our bishop when some chest pain and a four-hour ambulance ride changed my schedule for a while. We had hours of footage shot, but it all ended with the desks being loaded in a semi-trailer and heading for the docks in New Orleans.

The project lurked in the back of my mind for a few years, as I wasted time earning a living, but we finally made a connection with a group in Haiti called Living Media

International. It had started with a young artist from Iowa who'd moved to Haiti to do, you know, art. He'd settled in with some Haitian friends in the hills above Jacmel and worked seriously on his painting for a while, until a non-governmental organization (NGO) from somewhere in the United States started a school in the neighborhood. The school was badly needed and welcomed, but after a while the NGO decided they didn't want to run a school, that an orphanage would be cooler. They pulled the plug on the school funding and used their money someplace trendier.

No, seriously, they did.

Religious organizations do stupid things all the time. It can be a challenge to one's Christianity. And that's without bringing up the Crusades and the Salem Witch Trials. One of my favorite things about being a Methodist is that we've never actually burned anyone at the stake for anything.

At least, not yet.

So Lee and his buddies took over the school, because if they didn't do it, no one else was going to do it.

I loved their story right from that point, because I know the feeling of getting involved in some project for no better reason than that if I don't do it, it won't get done.

My wife and I planned a trip to Haiti, and my sister and her husband decided to come along. My sister is a public health nurse, her husband Joe is a videographer who speaks French, and my wife projects a bubble of congeniality that make all in the vicinity like her, and that good will occasionally spills over onto me. So, in all honesty, even though it was my idea I was probably the least necessary person on the trip.

We landed in Port Au Prince with a fortune in videography gear and three desks, disguised as luggage. It was a year after the big earthquake and things were still a mess.

That's not completely accurate. I've been in nearly twenty countries over four decades and Port Au Prince after the earthquake was by far the worst place I'd ever been. If there was a worse place on Earth, I didn't want to see it.

We made our way through customs and a gauntlet of Haitians trying to make money from us. On the other side were Angelica, the young woman who had provided our connection to Living Media, and a friend of hers with a Toyota pickup. We crawled in the back of the truck and headed out of town. It took a while, but we finally left behind baby blue tents, shattered buildings, and drifts of polystyrene food clamshells.

The country is lovely. Sure, the evidence of ecological devastation is everywhere, with land eroded down to bedrock and tethered goats nibbling on sparse vegetation. It's also easy to see the enormous effort and expense that's gone into trying to restore a damaged land.

The benches in the back of the pickup were made of 2x6s, but sadly my rear end needs something about twice as wide. I was uncomfortable fairly quickly and in actual pain four hours later when we pulled into Jacmel and ended up down by a beautiful beach, eating goat kabobs and trying to make a plan for our visit.

Late in the afternoon we went up into the mountains above the city to the community of Mizac. Not a city, not even a town, but a region, a collection of houses and a market, and around 35,000 people. There was no electricity or running water, at that time, and no hospital or doctor. There were a few solar powered street lights, but beyond that the darkness was complete. We chugged up a steep red dirt road and stumbled to beds in different houses.

The next morning dawned clear and bright. I was in a beautiful place.

That's my usual reaction to almost every place I go, (with the exception of Port Au Prince after the earthquake, and parts of Wall Street). I confess to an unseemly streak of PollyAnna in my makeup. Like most people, I can enjoy most conversations, and usually enjoy wherever I am. Not speaking the language was stressful, and the rules of society were different and impenetrable enough in the short time we were there that I was pretty much always edgy. But I'm used to that—I find most societal rules impenetrable and I'm used to being places where I'm not quite sure what's going on.

In many ways, Mizak, Haiti, was the beginning of this book. Lovely people, beautiful place and just so … screwed. Haiti is a terrific example of how to do everything wrong for centuries. We don't know who the original settlers of Haiti were, because Arawak migrants moving across the Caribbean from South America wiped them out by about A.D. 600. Columbus stopped by in 1492, and within 20 years the indigenous population was essentially extinct, wiped out by European diseases for which they had no resistance. A third of all Africans sold into slavery ended up in Haiti because the conditions were so brutal that it required importation of 10,000 to 15,000 people a year just to maintain the population. By 1789 there were 500,000 slaves, ruled by 30,000 Europeans.

But, it was an incredibly valuable possession—this one small island produced more sugar and coffee than all of Britain's West Indian colonies together. Of course, that moment in the sun was followed by 300 years of oppression, revolutions, bad weather, earthquakes and bad government, sometimes all of them simultaneously.

We talk about Post Traumatic Stress Disorder (PTSD) for military folks and survivors of terrorist attacks. Those people do have my profound sympathies, but imagine the PTSD when you live in a place where there have been almost unimaginable catastrophes in every generation for 300 years.

I've always had the feeling that if you could fix Haiti, you could fix anyplace. That's stupid, of course, because every country is different, with different issues, priorities, and challenges. But, just as there are some commonly accepted techniques for brain surgery and transmission repairs, there are some common threads for economic development work.

First, corruption is a killer. Things don't work well in a corrupt society. There's just too much friction. For instance, twenty years ago, back when this was real money, I spent $100,000 on a used tractor, sight unseen, based on the salesman's word that it was in good shape. I didn't see it until the day it was delivered. If I were in Haiti or fifty other countries around the world I would never do that. I wouldn't make the deal unless my brother-in-law the mechanic had checked the tractor out and signed off on its quality. Even then I'd be worried that the salesman had slipped him a few bucks for a bogus report.

When you add up all the effort that goes into not being cheated, it's just sand in the gears of progress. Nothing really gets done.

For instance, no one recommends mailing a letter to Haiti. The concern is that if it looks valuable it will be stolen, and if it doesn't it will be thrown away because it's too much bother to deliver. That's just one small example.

Second, the government is always part of the problem or part of the solution. Governments are just too pervasive, the elephant in the garage, causing ripples with every lurch or leap. Too much regulation is strangling, too little lets the strong dominate the weak, and ineffective regulation just leaves everyone cynical and frustrated.

Third, education is the silver bullet, and education of girls is a silver bullet with glitter and magic dust on it. Want to pick a decent country to live in? If women are educated and free to make their own decisions you should be willing to bet money that society there is relatively decent.

Haiti is a badly wounded society. It is a bleeding heart liberal's worst nightmare of a welfare society—there has been so much meddling from the outside, stretching back hundreds of years, and so much financial aid given the past few decades that it's hard to propagate an entrepreneurial attitude. You see huge numbers of idle, able-bodied adults, and a nearly infinite amount of work that needs to be done. An economist named Angus Deaton, who won a Nobel Prize in his field, has a theory that too much foreign aid hurts a country, just as countries that are rich in oil, diamonds, and other natural resources tend to do worse economically than countries with fewer tangible assets. Think of the differences between the Republic of Congo and Singapore.

> Education of girls is a silver bullet with glitter and magic dust on it.

His theory is that when there is too much free money floating around, from diamond mines or foreign aid, a government doesn't need to win the support of the people, the way it would if it needed to be supported by tax money.

I don't know if Dr. Deaton is right—I'm no economist and the last prize I won was for "Best Humorous Article," awarded by the American Agricultural Editors Association—but I'd be willing to bet he has a point. As a guy who's spent most of his life scrambling to pay the bills, it can be intensely frustrating dealing with both the recipients of and the distributers of aid.

About a year ago I was visiting with a guy who had made drilling wells in developing countries his mission.

We talked a little and he told me how his plan was to start an NGO and go around drilling wells wherever they were needed. I suggested that they sell their drill rig to a local guy. He could pay it off by drilling wells for free one day a week. The rest of the time he could work on his own and charge what the market would bear. I thought it was a solid idea—since he was getting the drill rig for free, except for his labor, he could keep his costs down and the people who couldn't afford anything could get in line for the once a week freebies. It just seemed to me like a small way to start some real, sustainable development going, with a chance for jobs, income, and no children dying of water-borne diseases. That seemed like a win.

The man looked at me as if I were speaking Urdu, (which, when you think about it, is a goofy saying, because there are around 100 million people who do speak Urdu). He explained to me, again, how he had a plan to start an NGO, bring volunteers over from America to spend a couple weeks at a time drilling wells for worthy and/or dying people. Let me repeat this again: If you're doing mission work and you're not planning to work yourself out of a job, I think you're doing it wrong.

I got the same sort of look, only from the other side, when I was trying to run with another idea. The way many small NGO's get stuff to their projects in places like Haiti or Sierra Leone is to band together until they have enough goods to fill a shipping container. After the container clears customs, the people at missions within the country are notified to come and pick up their stuff. Middlemen handle the shipping and notifications, with varying degrees of success. I know of at least one shipping company that pocketed all the shipping and processing costs, left the shipping containers on the dock in Miami, and then skipped town with the money.

I proposed that we become one of those middlemen—only, you know, an honest one—shipping the supplies our projects needed in a container with other people's supplies, then handling the distribution when it arrived in Haiti. Done properly it would lower our shipping costs and start a small business in Haiti, one that could possibly grow into something substantial, provide jobs and get some economic activity started.

There was a language barrier, and a cultural barrier, and I was trying to line it up from a long way away, but I was very disappointed because I simply had no confidence that the guys I knew in Haiti really understood what I was trying to do.

I finally just gave up.

Don't get me wrong. I'm not saying that no one works in Haiti, or that there aren't many folks creating businesses and jobs. What I'm saying is that for a significant portion of the population the habits of looking for help to come from somewhere else seem to have become ingrained. Another problem is that, despite staggering evidence to the contrary, there is an impulse to assume that people from First World countries know what we're talking about.

The best example I saw of this was that on our visit some folks brought their son to see our host. He had a bad infection in his leg and huge swelling. Our host was an art major at Iowa State, with a small first aid kit in his house. He knew more than I do about medical stuff, but not that much more. Yet all eyes turned to him.

I can't imagine the pressure on his part to perform.

I think that mission teams, instead of getting matching t-shirts with clever slogans on them should instead get t-shirts that read, "We aren't that smart. What do you think we should do?" It would just be truth in advertising.

And what's maddening, truly maddening, is that everywhere I've gone, and Haiti is no exception, when you move with the people who are struggling, the ones whose kids aren't educated, where health care and ambition are scanty, it's impossible not to think of the waste. How many potential Hemingways, Einsteins, or Picassos live a life that doesn't come fully to fruition? How many Mary Annings or Marie Curies are wasting their time hauling water and dodging militias instead of advancing the cause of science? How many machinists, veterinarians, and teachers never get the education they need to move into productive and prolonged employment?

That's what the "lifeboat is already full, let the rest drown," people are missing. Development work is in our own best interests.

We live in a world with eight billion other people. We need them all working at full throttle and totally engaged in order for us to achieve new things, improve what we have, and do what is needed. Anything less than that is unacceptable.

Lesson 11
Everything Old is New Again

During a planning and zoning meeting concerning the licensing of a new quarry, an employee of the quarry company tried to assuage the concerns of some local citizens around the desecration of the land by saying that in a hundred years when the quarry was exhausted it could be converted into a recreation area.

At the time, I thought it was a particularly dumb argument, but then I went to Wales.

I didn't know much about Wales before we went. I knew about a third of my ancestry came from there, and by and large it was the pain-in-the-neck third.

I loved Wales. The love grew slowly. One of our daughters had insisted we go to Conwy. We arrived in the middle of a particularly busy day, with stalled traffic and no place to park. We drove aimlessly inside the medieval town for a bit and I, exhausted by the need to stay on the left and not run over pedestrians, surrendered and headed across the river to Llandudno, where we had a place to stay.

That was worse—the traffic was heavier and the pedestrians were slower. I felt a little better when a parking spot opened up and I perfectly executed my first left-handed parallel park. The town was a little disconcerting—it was as if Las Vegas had been built by Queen Victoria.

We were on the top floor, up many stairs, of an old hotel, facing a not very attractive beach. My wife loves the ocean and we ended up walking the beach where we found no pretty shells, but a few squishy jellyfish. It didn't seem like a fair trade. We walked out a long and decaying pier, protecting our ice cream cones from rampaging sea gulls, then retired early.

Everyone we met was really kind of lovely. There were simply far too many of them for my taste.

The next morning we skipped our hearty, full Welsh breakfast and were at Conwy at the crack of dawn. We found it to be a magical place. This confirmed my opinion that the main problem with most tourist attractions is, you know, tourists.

We found an unlocked gate, climbed the decaying stairs and walked along the crest of the city wall as the sun was coming up, bathing the castle in lovely morning light. Feeling much better about the world, we left the crowded coast while everyone else was still digesting their baked beans, mushrooms, and sausages.

The National Slate Museum is located at Dilfach Ddu. No, that isn't a typo. I was, and am, endlessly amused by the Welsh language. If my life depended on deciphering a bit of Welsh text I'd just shrug and smile, because I could spend the rest of my life studying and never crack the code.

I actually think there is no Welsh language. I think it's the world's longest running practical joke. The Welsh people just arrange letters in random sequences and then convince all the non-Welsh there is meaning behind them. If you're walking down a street in Wales as people are coming home from work and you hear bursts of laughter coming from behind curtained windows, that's what the giggles are about. It's just the celebration of another day of fooling the chumps.

For hundreds of years Wales was a place where the people had two main avocations—raising sheep and killing invaders. Wales has more castles per capita than any place on earth, and most of the castles were built to protect the inhabitants from the locals. We weren't coming as invaders, so everyone was just lovely to us.

Quite honestly, that's been our experience pretty much everywhere we've gone. Other than being mugged in Buenos Aires and getting kicked out of a clock shop in Geneva, almost everyone in the world we've crossed paths with has been a testament to the sweetness of the human race.

About two hundred years ago Wales had a boom of its own, called the Industrial Revolution. All of a sudden the slate, coal, and other minerals hidden in the mountains of Wales were of profound importance and value.

As usual in a boom, three things happened. First, most of the money went someplace else. Second, there was a big influx of people looking for a decent living, and third no one cared very much what happened to the land as the wealth was extracted.

Now, I understand that extractive industries are needed. Without them, without the iron, coal, and other minerals, we'd all be sheepherders. Society made the choice against that hundreds of years ago. The issue goes back to my "booms are stupid" theory. Whenever there's a race to exploit something new, bad things happen.

The population in Wales quadrupled from 1801 to 1901, but the next fifty years saw a huge drop in industries like coal, slate, and iron. Most of the profits went to other places, and the only things that remained were the residents and the mess.

In 1966 a huge pile of coal mining waste placed above the town of Aberfan collapsed in a soggy landslide and buried an elementary school. One hundred sixteen children, almost half the children in the village, and 28 adults were killed. Like most industrial disasters it was completely avoidable and happened because the people who made the money didn't need to care about the workers.

Once again, government is always part of the problem or part of the solution. Ordinary people need someone to stand between them and greed. The argument you hear so often these days is between those people who want bigger government and those who want smaller. It's a stupid debate, because both sides should just unite and demand *competent* government.

After the disaster, there was an investigation called the "Davis Inquiry." Here's a terrific excerpt from the conclusion:

> We reject out of hand Mr. Ackner's observation that what has been revealed here is "callous indifference" by senior National Coal Board officials to fears of the tip-slide expressed to them. Callousness betokens villainy, and in truth there are no villains in this harrowing story. In one way, it might possibly be less alarming if there were, for villains are few and far between. But the Aberfan disaster is a terrifying tale of bungling ineptitude by many men charged with tasks for which they were totally unfitted, of failure to heed clear warnings, and of total lack of direction from above. Not villains, but decent

men, led astray by foolishness or by ignorance
or by both in combination, are responsible for
what happened at Aberfan …

There aren't that many evil people in the world, but
huge numbers of evil acts occur all the time. In case you've
skipped the rest of the book, booms are stupid and government needs to work.

Wales now is a wonderful, magical place. It's the people, the landscape, the history, but oddly enough, it's also
the remains of the Industrial Revolution. There are ropes
courses and zip lines in abandoned mines, and there are
the canals.

A couple of hundred years ago the United Kingdom
was the first country to be linked by a system of canals.
Pre-railroad and pre-highway, the beginning of the Industrial Revolution demanded a better means of transport
than a few donkeys or packhorses. Canals were built all
over the region, but within a few decades were superseded
by railroads. One problem is that the canals were very
narrow, with locks set at a standard of 7 feet 6 inches wide.
In mainland Europe the canals went through a moderniza-
tion process, widening and deepening them, but in the UK
most of the canals were owned by the railroads, and they
saw no point in improving what they saw as competition.
Abandoned and forgotten, the canals were seen as a blight
and a bother. About fifty years ago, groups of volunteers
started rebuilding them to use for recreational purposes so
now the canals have become a significant tourist attraction.

My wife and I picked up my sister and her husband at
the airport in Bristol and headed for Crickhowell. We left
Crickhowell towards Llangynidr, crossed over the river
bridge, turned right towards Talybont on Usk, went up a
hill and there we were, at Country Craft Narrowboats on

the Monmouth and Brecon Canal. We walked up a slight rise and saw a beautiful red boat bobbing gently in a slender canal, with a mossy stone lock oozing water a few feet upstream. Think Winnebago, except built like Katherine Hepburn, and floating. We received about a half hour of instruction and then the owner rode along with us until we'd made it through the first lock. After that we were on our own.

It was … swell. Seriously, it was the closest I've come to relaxed in 20 years. The canal is only twenty feet wide so you can't really get lost, and the canal boats only go three miles an hour so no matter how stupid you are, there's a limit to the amount of damage you can do.

We puttered along through the lovely countryside, stopping every now and then to eat and drink too much at any number of little pubs.

It was startling to think that a hundred years ago this had been the equivalent of an interstate highway, full of boats shipping slate roofing tiles, iron ore, and coal. The countryside had been transformed from quiet pastures to something approaching an industrial wasteland, with a flood of immigrants and eager-to-oppress industrilists. The locals had to make the transition from herding sheep and killing Englishmen to punching a time clock. After a hundred years of that, their descendants had to make another painful transition to a new world built on the bones of the past.

> Sometmes a complete reinvention is the only way to go.

However difficult it was, they've certainly arrived at a wonderful place. It was after this trip that I first read about New York's Highline park, built above the rooftops on an abandoned rail line, and then received a briefing on an ATV course set up in an abandoned gravel pit.

The examples are all around, so I finally had to concede that the quarry company wasn't completely daft.

People get comfortable, and the average organization and municipality could easily put "We Fear Change," on their letterhead, but the truth is, the world changes, and pretty rapidly at that. Sticking with the old and familiar may be warming, but sometimes a complete reinvention is the only way to go.

Lesson 12
Put Way Too Much Skin in the Game

I didn't want to go to Haiti, but I really didn't want to go to Uganda. Sadly, it's been my experience that when I go to a place I have no desire to go to, that's where I do my best journalism.

All I really knew about Uganda was Idi Amin. He's been dead for a decade and was out of the country for a quarter of a century before his death, so I probably should let that go.

I belong to the International Federation of Agricultural Journalists. The federation works with an organization called Agriterra, which does economic development work in Africa. The group was planning a tour of Uganda with a selected group of international journalists to look at some of the projects there. Since I knew nothing about Africa it seemed like a golden opportunity to educate myself. I applied and was accepted. I was pretty proud of myself for being accepted, since there was basically only one person per country eligible, but then someone pointed out that there might not be that many people who wanted to take a bus tour of rural Ugandan farming enterprises.

I didn't really do much preparation for the trip. A few weeks before my flight I noticed a lump in a previously non-lumpy portion of my body, and went to the doctor to get it checked out. He diagnosed a hernia and referred me to a surgeon. The surgeon examined me and said the previous diagnosis was in error—I didn't have a hernia, I had a double hernia. He recommended surgery. I suggested that I wait until after my return.

He said, "Okay, but you might want to consider the chances of an emergency operation for a strangulated intestine in the back country of Uganda."

I thought that was a solid point. The bottom line is that instead of working out and doing research, I spent a substantial portion of my pre-trip time laying on the couch and whining.

The whining didn't stop when I left, either. It's a lot of bother to get from western Minnesota to Kampala. The way I did it was to drive for four hours to Minneapolis, get on a plane to Newark, then Brussels, than Kigali, and finally Kampala thirty hours later.

I was sort of hoping I'd have to fight my way through a flock of giraffes to get to the luggage carousel, but it turns out the airport in Kampala is just like every other airport I've ever been in.

Okay, that's not entirely true. First I landed in the darkness of the Ugandan night and was transported through crowded streets and berserk traffic to the hotel in Kampala. It was an hour's journey of pot-holed roads, motorbikes with no tail-lights, and ten thousand suicidal pedestrians strolling down the places where the non-existent shoulders of the road should be.

It took a couple of days before we made it out into the countryside. When we did, I was charmed beyond words.

Everywhere we went there were beautiful, healthy, smiling children. In my life, I've seen too many photos of starving children and I'd been dreading the sight in person, but where we went there was plenty of food. In general, throughout the world, starvation results from the unfair distribution of food, not the lack of it. The people were very gracious and welcoming, although on the last day we got far enough up in the hills that some of the little kids appeared to be unfamiliar with white people. At least that's what I'm telling myself.

When the bus stopped and I climbed out, a cluster of small children took one horrified look at me and ran away screaming. Granted, I hadn't been sleeping very well, but I'm choosing to believe it wasn't my appearance per se that upset them, just an unfamiliarity with my skin tone.

Not only was I the wrong color, I was the wrong age. Only two percent of people in Uganda are over the age of 65. It's a place where you can raise enough food for a family on an acre and a half, but if a member of that family gets an infection or even a relatively mild disease, it can be a death sentence.

You can get your meals off the banana tree in the backyard, but when I went to buy cough drops, the clerk opened the box, picked up a pair of scissors and asked how many I wanted. When I offered to take the whole box, she looked at me as if I were a billionaire. Living as I do in the easy part of the world, it was stunning to have it rubbed in my face just how difficult and fragile life can be. Granted, the AIDs epidemic had a lot to do with changing the demographic picture in Uganda, but it wasn't the whole story.

In all honesty, I expected to come home discouraged. I've been in some hard, sad, places in my life, places where it is difficult to see a road forward. That was not my feeling in Uganda, not at all. There is so much potential there; rich land, hard-working people, and an entrepreneurial spirit. Of course, there were also far too many men sitting idly by the side of the road watching the traffic go by, and too much meddling from an inconsistent and often corrupt government.

It's exciting, but also frustrating, because you get the feeling that with just a little more luck and a little more hard work, they will go over the top toward a vastly brighter future. But that brighter future is by no means certain.

Sixteen of us made this trip. Between us, we were from eleven countries. We all brought our own experiences and prejudices, but in conversation I believe we all came to a common conclusion. Uganda, and Africa in general, are so close, so close to becoming a place that will lift up all of us.

Some of the fastest growing economies in the world are in Africa, and the only thing holding them back is government ineptitude. Perhaps I'm being generous. Sometimes it can be hard to differentiate ineptitude from active malevolence. If even a modest level of competence and caring from their politicians can be had, the sky's the limit.

And that's a good thing. As an American, I wish other countries well, but my heart is with my homeland. And America does better in a world full of strong, free societies. We shouldn't fear the prosperity of other nations; we should yearn for it. Every country that lifts more of its people into the middle class is another potential customer for the things America makes and grows.

I stated that Uganda was a mostly pleasant paradox. The climate is perfect, the people are wonderful, but metal detectors and guards with AK-47s are stationed in front of supermarkets. When I mentioned over lunch one day that I wanted to find something from Uganda to give my wife, a lady took a bracelet off her arm as a gift. Still, 90% of the ATMs didn't work and the roads varied from bumpy to horrendous.

One night, we attended a reception for a big bank that was receiving an award for making a large investment in economic development. An ambassador from the bank's home country showed up to present the award, and there were a few executives there to receive it. I watched three junior bankers standing off to one side, acting like teenagers at their first funeral—looking around and sharing giggles over one thing or another. They were grown men but at one point actually had to be shushed by their boss.

It made me grumpy. I wasn't enjoying myself at the presentation, but at least I had the common courtesy to review movie trailers in my head instead of being outwardly rude.

Later that evening, at a reception, one of my international colleagues who'd been out doing actual journalism came up to me, very indignant, and told me how he'd uncovered the fact that the big bank wasn't investing its money in the hinterland of rural Uganda, thus enriching the lives and futures of generations of hard working peasants, but instead had weaseled the award for spending money to refurbish their corporate headquarters.

I was less indignant for two reasons. First, I always expect the worst from any big bank. Second, I'd already decided the twerps in suits were assholes and it was nice to have my opinion confirmed.

In our tour we mainly looked at various agricultural cooperatives. They varied from brilliant to misled.

One of the brilliant examples was a small co-op that had obtained funding to buy a cooled bulk-tank for milk. Uganda is right on the Equator, which means that fresh milk becomes dangerous milk in a matter of hours. When we arrived at the co-op headquarters we found an assortment of scooters and bicycles with ten-gallon tins of milk strapped to their backs. The milk was checked for bacteria, then dumped in the tank to be chilled. In a different line, local folks with two-quart pitchers walked up to buy milk. Every couple of days a tanker would take the overage to a factory to be made into cheese.

No huge money making opportunity, just a small accumulation of profits and a larger payoff in healthy milk drinkers. It's the sort of thing I've noticed over the years—so many people are trying for a home run. Every now and then you do hit a home run, but more often than not you strike out. You're not going to see many banner headlines about the village in Uganda where children don't have chronic diarrhea, and a dairy farmer was able to buy a new bicycle. But it all adds up.

We went way up in the hills to tour two small coffee cooperatives. For me, this was perhaps the most interesting part of the trip. At the first one, we were greeted by their whole board of directors, with various official titles, all in matching t-shirts. Their small office had inspirational sayings pasted hither and yon, and everyone was very sincere. The only problem was that their coffee wasn't very good.

Most farms in Uganda have a coffee tree or two in the backyard, for their own consumption, and to pick up spending money. No problem with that, but there was just no way to gather beans from all those backyard trees and get consistent taste or quality on a large scale. And there was no way color-coordinated t-shirts were going to change that.

The next day we went further up in the hills. I was still hoping to see a band of gorillas stroll out of the brush, but it was all still farmland. Living as I do, in the very epicenter of the North American continent, you'd think I'd have an intuitive grasp of how big places can be, but apparently not.

One of my favorite stories involves working the room at a reception after a book thing. There was a guy from New York City chatting me up. About 8:00 p.m. I checked my watch and said, "Well, I gotta go, I have a four hour drive home."

He said, "Wow, where do you live?" I said, "Western Minnesota, near South Dakota."

He said, "Maybe this is a New York thing, but I have no idea where South Dakota is." I let that pass, because I'm trying to be a better person, but then he went on to say, "I changed planes in Sioux Falls, and I thought as long as I was this close, I should probably run over and see Mount Rushmore."

I'm in favor of people seeing Mount Rushmore, and it is in South Dakota, but it's four hundred miles from Sioux Falls. I said, "Yeah, you should. Next time you're in Sioux Falls airport just pop out the door and ask the first cab to take you to Mount Rushmore."

I thought I was pretty clever, but a couple years later I was telling that story while giving a speech in South Dakota and someone from the audience yelled, "You should have told him to take the subway."

Dammit. Oh, what I wouldn't give for a time machine.

Even with all the driving we did, the closest we ever got to a gorilla was three hundred miles. And Uganda is one of the smaller countries in Africa.

So, when we were up in the hills I didn't see any wildlife other than Grey Crowned cranes, but I did see a coffee cooperative that left me hopeful. There were no matching t-shirts here, but the director was a guy who'd been working in business for a few decades and had traveled enough to figure out what people wanted. And what people want is to order a cup of coffee and have it taste they way they want it to taste, every time. This particular co-op had been ruthless about making all their members plant the same kind of coffee tree. Furthermore, coffee beans don't all ripen at the same time, so to do things just right you need to harvest each crop a half dozen times. These folks were trying to do things just right. After our stroll through the coffee plantation we had some samples made for us, on a table festooned with awards the co-op has won.

I don't know for sure which one of these cooperatives is going to prosper, but in the words of Damon Runyon, "The race isn't always to the swift, nor the battle to the strong, but that's the way to bet." There is an element of luck in any success story, and everyone needs some luck. But almost the only thing I learned in college was from an offhand comment by a professor who said, "I believe in good luck, and I've had my share of it, but I've found that the harder I work, the more good luck comes my way."

I've never really heard better advice than that. By and large, people really want small, struggling farmers and cooperatives to prosper, but good intentions and good will are aided mightily by competence and performance.

The bus finally took us back to Kampala. Our hotel was located on the other side of the city from the Entebbe airport. It's a trip that takes somewhere between a half hour and four hours depending on the traffic. Our leader had the brilliant idea for us to go very early and then have a long, relaxed dinner within sight of the airport. We sat on a patio overlooking Lake Victoria. The food was good, the conversation pleasant, and the weather perfect.

There was only one flaw in the evening, something that bothers me so much I've never talked about it. At the next table were a couple of pudgy young men dressed in khakis and polo shirts. The assumption at my table was that they were Americans, probably because most of the world is always willing to believe the worst about Americans. With them at the table were two beautiful young women—way overdressed for the time and venue.

I live on a farm outside a very small town in western Minnesota and I've been in a monogamous relationship since 1973. What I don't know about sex workers is, well, everything. Maybe my group's assumptions were completely wrong. Let's face it—if loutish young men weren't occasionally able to attract the attention and approval of young women the human race would have died out centuries ago.

The men were drinking a lot and, here's the part that really bothered me, the young women were eating a lot. Not date eating, nibbling on a small salad with a glass of white wine. No, they both ordered a big meal and ate it as if they were really hungry.

I've said I didn't see starving people in Uganda, but keep in mind we spent most of the time in the rural areas. The two young women we saw, getting a decent meal any way they could, seemed symbolic of something I've seen play out on six continents over six decades. When you live in a small place, you have for better or worse, a measure of autonomy and independence. You might not have any money, but you can raise a garden, and keep some goats or hunt for rabbits. If your lights go out, your first move isn't to call the power company. Most rural people I know try to diagnose the problem themselves.

As soon as your life becomes more urban, you need to start relying on other people for the basic necessities of life. And the real kicker is that for decades, perhaps centuries, the best way to advance yourself has been to leave the rural areas, head for the big city, and take the chance that society will help you out if needed.

My wife and I were once on the island of Utsira, off the coast of Norway, working on a story about a wind turbine project that Norske Hydro was working on. A rock wall that appeared to serve no useful purpose stretched across the island. Our host explained that during the Great Depression folks from the larger towns received food from the farmers. To preserve everyone's pride, the city folks took the food in exchange for building the wall. No one mentioned that the wall wasn't really needed.

For a few thousand years, Norwegian peasants had been able to ignore depressions and recessions, living an autonomous life (if they could avoid getting drafted into a king's army). Civilization requires cities, and cities mean you have to depend on many other people for the requirements of daily living, and you need to shell out actual cash for many of those items.

Then you risk building a wall to nowhere or selling your body and soul for food to eat.

I've seen the same thing in places as far apart as Detroit, Port Au Prince and, apparently, Kampala. The country empties out so families can get an education and a future for their children. If things don't work out, they're stuck. Instead of living on beans and side pork they raised themselves, now they're dependent on the dole, or worse, to keep their family fed. This is the mortal sin of governance, the betrayal of the people who are depending on you to keep the wheels on the wagon.

When it came time to leave, the restaurant's credit card machine wasn't working. By this point in the trip, within sight of the airport in a country where you can't easily get the money exchanged into your home currency, not everyone had cash. The restaurant manager was determined to get paid. I thought a reasonable point could be that we'd asked the manager if he accepted credit cards before we sat down, so if he didn't get paid because his equipment malfunctioned, tough noogies.

That seemed like a more nuanced argument than I wanted to make in a foreign country with an uncertain justice system and a plane leaving that I very much wanted to get on. Since, as always, I live in Worst Case Scenario World I still had plenty of cash and paid for three or four dinners, and a couple of my colleagues paid for the rest.

We made it to the airport on time, sailed through security, and still had time to kill, leading to those awkward encounters where you've said heartfelt goodbyes in the parking lot, followed by running into the same people in the gift shop while waiting for the plane to load.

After another long flight I landed in Brussels and found the connecting flight to Newark. When I got in line to load I was informed that I was in line for the wrong flight from Brussels to Newark.

Truthfully, I had no idea there would be two planes leaving simultaneously from Brussels for Newark, which I suppose just goes to show how sheltered I am.

I raced five gates down, not even having enough time to figure out a story to make missing the plane not my fault, clambered aboard, and found my seat. We took off in a couple of minutes and headed west.

What did I learn? I learned, again, that I don't like traveling without my wife. She typically is the one who carries the tickets and passports, along with treats so I don't whine on the plane. More importantly, whenever I see something cool when she's not along my first thought is, "Robin would love this." For instance, most of the little kids I saw had their heads shaved, which seems like a genius idea, and the vision of my wife sitting cross legged on the grass with a gaggle of bald headed six year olds wearing school uniforms in her lap (and she always ends up with children in her lap) is entrancing.

I suppose I could say I learned that continents and colors don't matter so much, but that's a lesson I've been learning for several decades. Three of my five grandchildren are from Ethiopia so in the past decade I've developed a fondness for the African continent that is very personal, as opposed to run of the mill do-gooder's well wishes.

Having said that, on the long list of sayings that annoy me, "Oh, I don't even see color," is well towards the top of the list. Of course I see color. I'm glad of it—my grandchildren are all beautiful, and their colors, which range from nearly transparent to pink to a rich black, are part and parcel of their beauty. This is so simple, it makes me howl with frustration that the human race at large doesn't quite seem to grasp that people are individuals and need to be loved or loathed as individuals, not due to their membership in some particular demographic.

I'm opposed to the death penalty, because I think that governments in general are bad at killing people properly. That sounds sort of noble to say, but I own a backhoe and a shotgun, and if it weren't for general societal disapproval there would be a number of freshly dug holes on my farm. Perhaps that's why we have the rule of law and not of men, and perhaps that's why general assumptions about any group are a bad idea.

Another thing I learned or re-learned is how we can't ignore government. At the risk of repeating myself, government is always part of the problem or part of the solution. I've never seen a place where the role of government was unimportant. Working for good governance is a bother, because by and large people get the government they deserve.

Delivering food by Humvee to starving people is so much more rewarding than explaining to a first time village council why "Robert's Rules of Order" matter. But most of the people in the history of the world who have starved to death have done so because they lived with a crappy government, not because there wasn't enough food available in the world.

> If you don't have way too much skin in the game, you won't put in the effort to really succeed.

Next, carefully crafted mission statements and nifty uniforms are no substitute for competence and hard work. You can be as cute as a big-eyed kitty herding baby chicks, with a need that calls for a telethon and an idea that screams, "Kickstarter!" but at some point you'll actually need to do the work. If you don't have the desperation of having way too much skin in the game you won't put in the effort to really succeed.

I'm no expert on Africa. In a week I saw a tiny corner of Uganda, and Uganda is a tiny corner of the continent. But that trip is the one that gave me the confidence to write this book, because I was able to recognize the themes that I feel lead to success, and failure.

Lesson 13
Look for Solutions from Left to Right

Go down the stairs to the basement in the Big Stone County Courthouse. Take a left and walk past the Veteran's Service Officer and Human Resources. You'll come to the Commissioners' Room. The county commissioners meet there a few times a month—the rest of the time it serves as a meeting place with a dozen chairs and an ITV setup.

Inside the room is a long, beat up desk with seven comfortable chairs behind it. During meetings the county attorney sits on one end, and the county auditor sits on the other. The commissioners take turns as Chair, one year at a time, so our alignment changes every twelve months.

This year I'm seated at the far left, with our most conservative member at the far right, and the others in between, more or less perfectly aligned as regards where we fit on the political spectrum. When someone noticed that we had a good laugh, after which we moved through our agenda, paying the bills, planning how to cope with upcoming retirements, and passing a motion to buy a new road grader.

There's a lot we don't agree on, but those issues very seldom come up. Part of the reason for this is that providing basic services, where the rubber meets the road, shouldn't really be a partisan issue. I know it turns into a partisan issue on a state and national level, but it shouldn't. Another piece is our ability to frame the discussion. For instance, my most conservative colleague hates spending taxpayer's money. For my part, I'm more of a bleeding heart liberal.

Actually, that's not accurate. I'm not so much bleeding heart liberal as bleeding heart libertarian. If that's not a thing, it should be. On the one hand, I hate telling people what to do as much as I hate being told what to do, and I have a profound distrust of government. On the other hand, I've seen over and over that there are some problems that simply require collective action to solve.

As opposed to my conservative colleague, I have no problem with spending taxpayers' money, I just want it spent as carefully as possible, because that means we can do more with it.

> Some problems simply require collective action to solve.

What that means is that the far left and the far right at the commissioners' table are often combining to be the most ruthless in terms of holding groups accountable for how carefully they're spending other people's money. As a lefty, cleaning up the water and preventing erosion are personal priorities to me, but if the argument is framed such that a cleaner lake makes for better economic development, there is common ground to be found there as well.

It's not quite as simple as it sounds, and there are real differences in philosophy and priorities, but the end result is that things get done, which is what the taxpayers expect.

The day after we discovered the ideological alignment of our chairs in the Commissioners' Room there was a 7:00 a.m. meeting of the Clinton-Graceville-Beardsley School Foundation Committee at the café. Seven people came through the door. They were all people I know, and politically they were about as diverse as you could be and not be shooting at each other. But they all have kids, and they all want those kids to have a decent education. That's a solid starting point. Ferocious Facebook discussions about religion and politics appeared to be left at the door, submerged by higher priorities.

This is one of the profound benefits of living in a small place. Marc Dunkelman, a research fellow at Brown University, has written a book called "The Vanishing Neighbor." In it he makes the case that one of the transformations of American life is that we have hundreds of acquaintances on Facebook and other social media, but very few friends. The friends we do have tend to be people who think and act just like us. In my small town the banker plays racquetball with the school janitor, and the superintendent discusses basketball with a carpenter and a retired farmer over eggs and bacon. Mr. Dunkelman's point is that those cross-cultural contacts are what make discussion, negotiation, and compromise possible.

You get used to not spouting off because the Neanderthal neighbor with the appalling political views also is the guy who gave your daughter a ride home after she had a flat tire, and his wife was the one who wrote the lovely note to your nephew when he was in rehab. Of course, the downside of all this is you spend all your time just getting along, when in fact there are moments when you really should plant your feet firmly and say, "Here I stand. God help me, I can do no other."

For the sake of your sanity, those moments probably shouldn't come along very often.

Reflections

This is the last chapter of the book. Every book I've written, this is the part where I begin to panic. As a writer, I'm working with a multi-generational inferiority complex. A few years ago, one of my cousins went to Norway to investigate our lineage, traced it back about 500 years, and discovered five centuries of peasants. There's nobody famous, nobody who mattered, certainly no one whose opinion has ever been sought out by, well, anyone.

All those generations of anonymous, honorable, ignored ancestors loom behind me as I write.

They're not comfortable companions.

I'm writing this on a cold January day. I'm sitting in my empty café two hours after closing, just killing time, because at 3:30 I'm going to be helping eight 4th Grade Girl Scouts with their cooking merit badge. My plan is to make quiche and crepes and show them how to flip an egg in a frying pan without using a spatula. I don't know if that's enough for a merit badge, but it's all I've got.

One thing about January in Minnesota, it is prime time for introspection.

I've been trying to decide if this project has been worth it. All told the Bush Foundation invested about $100,000 in me. After I sent in my final report I waited a while for the letter saying they wanted their money back, but none appeared. Too late now.

Of course, it wasn't just the Bush Foundation who paid. I paid myself a thousand dollars a month out of the Foundation's funds for the first two years, nothing for the next two. Granted, I didn't get into this for the money, and I haven't been starving, but working for free for long enough can make you feel like a chump.

The café is now up to code for the first time since 1927, and my customer base has swelled from two the first day to 40 to 50 on a busy day. I've created a couple of jobs, and perhaps helped keep another small business, (Bonnie's grocery store) open.

One entrepreneur made and sold 1,000 gallons of apple cider out of the facility, but the next year was a bad year for apples. Another guy has done the same thing with 300 gallons of sauerkraut. Last week a woman who has developed a cottage industry making homemade tortillas and tamales out of her home stopped by, and we discussed her doing that work here.

On the other hand, of the half-dozen people who said they yearned for a facility like this one for similar purposes, not one has come through the door. Perhaps if I weren't here they would like it better.

The local foods people, who set a goal of aggregating a million pounds of vegetables a year using this place as a hub, missed that goal by about six digits. A friend who I had some random conversations with about brewing beer in the back room died in a tragic accident. Another couple of people who made some hard cider that was a big success bought a defunct monastery, and now they are sinking their time and money into that. A family with a budding vineyard became bored with the process and decided to become missionaries in Guatemala.

I'm old enough that I'm not particularly surprised by any of these developments. It's been my experience that plans change and life happens.

A big surprise to me, and a fascinating one is, in my opinion, the apocalyptic views of so many of the local, fresh food folks. It's really interesting—I can't tell you how many conversations I've had with people who truly believe the downfall of civilization is just around the corner. They don't say it out loud, but they actually seem to be looking forward to it.

I think it's because when that dark day comes they'll have their windmills, greenhouses and compost piles ready to go, and they would need to be saints to not wish for the chance to say "I told you so" a few times.

I was talking to one guy who carefully explained his plans to move his family out to the back of beyond where no one would be able to find them. I suggested that perhaps it would make more sense to make yourself a member of a community of a few hundred people, so there would be a critical mass that would enable some specialization, such as blacksmiths and doctors. The conversation and the attitude made me a little crazy, because if history shows us anything, it shows us that we prosper when we bind together, not when we splinter apart.

> We prosper when we bind together, not when we splinter apart.

Of course, the Bush Foundation never actually cared that much about the café. They more or less saw it as a homework project for me, with the true success or failure of the project revolving around how much I developed in my chosen field. I have to say, the jury is probably still out on that one. I think the people running the program intended the Fellowship as a voyage of self-discovery. To that end, the other Fellows and I took personality profile tests, had retreats four times a year, and were even assigned life coaches to help us understand ourselves.

But here's the thing. I've spent a tremendous amount of time alone in my life, starting at a pretty early age. For the past twenty years I've been an essayist, meaning that every week I sit in front of a computer screen and spend hours and hours trying to decide exactly how I feel about a particular issue. Of course, the issues range from climate change to my wife's dog, but nevertheless, this is serious introspection time. In terms of public experience I was asked to run for the office of Soil and Water Conservation Supervisor in 1977, and ever since then I've been doing some sort of public service, paid and unpaid, on literally more boards and commissions than I can remember. I've worked for wages, I've met a payroll, and I've spent many millions of dollars of other people's money.

> Many of the really great ideas are the result of collaborative compromise.

While none of that actually means anything in particular, it does mean I've developed a pretty firm idea of what works and what doesn't, what matters and what doesn't. I've traveled about as far on a voyage of self-discovery as I'm willing to go.

For the past thirty-five thousand words or so I've been trying to decide just what I have learned. Actually, it's not that much.

I was a little bit startled to find that the first thing that comes to mind is how pointless rigid ideologies are. Ideas come from the edges, progress comes from the middle. Many of the really great ideas are the result of collaborative compromises. That's why our current governmental catastrophes are so damaging, because we function best when we duke it out in the public arena, taking and giving shots and finally angrily signing off on a jury-rigged compromise that satisfies no one, but sets our republic up to stagger down the road a few more decades.

> You need to work with people you can trust.

Next, you need to work with people you can trust. One of my son's favorite illustrations is from Ernest Hemingway's book, "A Moveable Feast." It's a memoir of Hemingway's early years in Paris. There's a chapter that chronicles his meeting with F. Scott Fitzgerald. At this point in time the literary world knew that Hemingway had some game, but Fitzgerald had just published "The Great Gatsby" and was considered a bigger deal. The two men hit it off, and Fitzgerald asked Hemingway if he wanted to take the train to the country to pick up a car Fitzgerald had left behind, then take a leisurely trip back.

To Hemingway this seemed like a tremendous opportunity, and he was eagerly waiting at the train station the next morning. Fitzgerald never showed up. Hemingway worried he'd been in an accident, that he'd misunderstood which train station, or that he had reconsidered. The truth was, Fitzgerald was still drunk and had completely forgotten about the commitment. In the book the next line was, "At this point in my life, I didn't know that a grown man could be late for a train."

My father had made the same point to me when I was in high school. I was fuming about a friend's failure to carry through on some plans. I said, "I could trust him with my life, but I couldn't trust him to pick me up at the bus on time." My father asked, "But what if your life depended on being picked up at the bus on time?"

At this point in my life, I've developed a raging intolerance of people who don't do what they say they'll do. If you let me down, you probably will never know how it bothers me, but in time you might notice that I never ask you for anything ever again. I don't have to agree on politics or your favorite music, but you have to do what you say you'll do.

> Do what you say you'll do. Embrace ambiguity. And ante up.

Learn to embrace ambiguity. The most difficult thing we do, as human beings, is to develop systems that deal with individuals. I believe in procedures and policies—they add clarity, fairness, and transparency to organizations, but people often hide behind policy in order to avoid making decisions.

Ante up. Without skin in the game, there aren't very many successes. You need that panic stricken feeling of having spent more than you can afford in order to make you put in the hours and effort to turn a good idea into a good business.

One of my all time favorite stories involves the golfer Lee Trevino. Before he became a success on the pro tour he hustled for grocery money at local golf courses. After he won a playoff for his first big tournament win he was asked if the pressure of making a shot for thousands of dollars had bothered him. "That's not pressure," he said. "Pressure is playing for five bucks a hole when you only have three dollars in your wallet."

That level of skin in the game is what it takes.

I'm writing these last few lines at my desk, late at night, while staring out the window at the bitter darkness of a January cold.

This morning Lester was in early, fretting because one of his hearing aids broke in half and he needed to get to the VA to get it fixed. Cal stopped by, a little worried because his son, a Lieutenant in the Army, is going to be deployed next year to someplace we wouldn't want to go. Four businesswomen who had to be at work at 8:00 a.m. came in at 7:30 a.m. for scrambled eggs, no toast, because of the carbs.

After 9:00 a.m. a few retirees with not quite enough to do had extra cups of coffee. Sometime during the morning a couple of highway refugees looking for a breakfast not involving convenience store food saw the café sign and came in. They were surprised to find good bread and decent coffee. I made a nearly perfect omelet, and at the end of the morning I only had one cup of coffee extra in the coffeemaker.

There was a meeting later in the day. I took muffins. We listened to a presentation about the recent demographic blip that shows people wanting to move to rural areas to raise their children, if they can find jobs and eat Thai food for lunch. It was all very encouraging, and it was fun to watch people chatter excitedly about the possibilities.

Although, it did make me feel a little old. In 1977 Dave Steen and Donnie Morrill stopped at my house and asked if I wanted to fill out an unexpired term on the Soil and Water Conservation Board. I ended up serving 12 years. Another 12 years on the Holy Trinity Hospital Board where I was the token Protestant. A couple of decades as a youth group leader, a member of the Big Stone County Pork Producers, a decade on the Board of Ordained Ministry of the United Methodist Church, Northern Growers Ethanol, Southwest Minnesota Arts and Humanities Council, Big Stone Wind, Big Stone Area Growth, three terms as a county commissioner … a lot of time struggling towards a future that now seems within grasp. It all makes me feel a little like Moses, seeing a Promised Land ahead, but being willing to sit under a tree and watch the others cross over without me.

When I closed I didn't clean the grill, but I did mop the floor and set out bread dough for tomorrow. Tomorrow Lester will probably be in for coffee at 6:15, and later in the morning 27 kindergartners are walking over from the school to have a treat. I don't know how much longer I'll be doing this, and I don't know what will happen to the place after I'm done.

But today, today was a good day.

The author, with his wife Robin, and their five grandchildren.

About the Author

Brent Olson has lived 60 of his 62 years on a small farm in Big Stone County, on the edge of the prairie in western Minnesota. His weekly column "Independently Speaking" is seen by a million people a week.

In this time of news and information tailored so everyone can hear only what they want to hear, he presents information that will leave everyone just a little unsettled. Working with a warm heart and a cold eye, he dissects what works from what doesn't in our individual lives, our institutions, and our country.

Olson put three children through college as a farmer, has experienced solid success and stunning failure as an entrepreneur, and as a journalist has filed stories from twenty countries.

He has served on dozens of boards and committees—as varied as the Big Stone County Pork Producers, and the Minnesota United Methodist Board of Ordained Ministry. In his time as a short order cook at his very own Inadvertent Café he has learned to make fluffy scrambled eggs, and the best omelets on Main Street in Clinton, Minnesota (Population 453).

Olson is a Big Stone County Commissioner and a 2012 Bush Foundation Fellow.